CRAZY FEBRUARY

CRAZY FEBRUARY

Death and Life
in the
Mayan Highlands of Mexico

by CARTER WILSON

UNIVERSITY OF CALIFORNIA PRESS
Berkeley, Los Angeles, London

University of California Press
Berkeley and Los Angeles, California

University of California Press, Ltd.
London, England

First Paperback Edition 1974
(Original hardcover edition [without subtitle] published 1966
by J. B. Lippincott Company)

ISBN: 0-520-02399-4
Library of Congress Catalog Card Number: 72-95309

Printed in the United States of America

7 8 9

CONTENTS

Introduction to the Paperback Edition   *1*

PART ONE / The President

1.	The Man Salvador	*13*
2.	Doctor Méndez	*27*
3.	The President	*40*
4.	Mario	*60*
5.	The Boy	*63*
6.	Juan López Oso	*74*
7.	Mario	*87*
8.	The President	*101*
9.	Juan López Oso	*112*
10.	Don Roberto	*115*

11.	Doctor Méndez at the Fountain of Desire	*125*
12.	Mario	*134*
13.	Juan López Oso	*145*
14.	Mario	*149*
15.	The President	*154*

PART TWO / Juan López Oso

16.	Juan López Oso	*163*
17.	Eliseo	*179*
18.	Mario	*184*
19.	The Curer	*186*
20.	The Maestro	*188*
21.	Miguel	*205*
22.	Don Alonso's Maid	*220*
23.	The Man Salvador	*223*
24.	Don Roberto	*224*
25.	Don Roberto's New Man	*229*
26.	Eliseo	*236*
27.	Second Alcalde	*245*

Glossary	*252*

Introduction to the Paperback Edition

> "Well, statements are the work of
> other men, the doctor decided.
> Especially statements about Indians."

Products of the "imagination," such as novels, can be especially useful tools for understanding how things work in societies far removed from our own experience. Through the telling of a story, a sound ethnographic novel conveys more than information. It involves the reader in the dynamics of life in places where the rules for action are very different from the rules the reader makes his own decisions by.

Some people believe ethnographic novels are comparable to fieldnotes—the data themselves in their original, unanalyzed form. Though I can see the reason for the analogy, I still disagree with it. Good fieldnotes record raw experience. For the time being, the anthropologist squelches his desire to interpret, and he writes down everything he can see or remember. Good ethnographic fiction also presents experience raw, without generalization. But in building the story, in selecting to tell *this* because it is important and not to tell *that* because it seems trivial, the novelist is analyzing his material. Between the raw and the cooked, both ethnographies and ethnographic novels belong in the processed pot.

Anthropologists try to make explicit and public both the method they have used to gather their material and the means for analyzing it. Ordinarily, a novelist obscures his analysis—the grounds for the choices he has made—and depends on the interior logic of the story to make his tale seem "true" or "believable." But in *Crazy February* I was working with somewhat different principles than I would normally use in writing "fiction." The book grew directly out of field experience. I felt strongly that it would stand or fall on its

ethnographic correctness. And so, faced with choices between what
I would like to see in the story and what I thought would actually
happen to an Indian in the mountains of Chiapas, I consistently
chose "actuality." In a practical, day-to-day writing sense, reality
was my rod and my staff. And in the end I was very happy when
anthropologists with greater experience in the Mayan area found the
book essentially exact and, more important, true to the spirit of the
place I had written about.

It now seems right that, as an anthropologist does, I should make
public something about how my fieldwork was accomplished.

Usually the direction and future course of my life is obscured from
me. So I am startled when I remember how clear were my reasons
for going to southern Mexico in June, 1963. I knew I wanted to write
novels. I was convinced that there must exist ways for a novelist to
sharpen his skills at observing the world at large. Karl Heider, a
friend and teacher just returned from work with the Dani in New
Guinea (now West Irian), suggested working with anthropologists,
who are trained to articulate and record precisely what they see.
Evon Z. Vogt, director of the Harvard Chiapas Project, then agreed
to take me on for a summer's apprenticeship in fieldwork. I meant to
gain experience and to learn techniques, and in exchange to give back
to the project whatever useful data I collected. I had no plan to write
any fiction about Indian Mexico.*

The spine of handsome, forested mountains which runs through
Chiapas into Guatemala has for a long time been a refuge and bastion
where Mayan Indians could maintain and elaborate a traditional
agricultural way of life. At the time of *Crazy February,* there were
about 200,000 speakers of the Mayan languages Tzotzil and Tzeltal
living in *municipios* (incorporated towns) in the country around the
small Mexican city of San Cristóbal Las Casas (San Martín in the
book).

The place I call "Chomtik" is in fact named Chamula. It is the
most populated of the Indian municipios (more than 30,000 inhabi-
tants) and the coldest, since it occupies the highest part of the
mountain range. People live in *parajes* (hamlets), with their corn-

---

* Rather than giving the usual list of acknowledgments, I point out here
  that the people mentioned in this short account, and many more, have
  been generous to me with their time, their resources, their friendships,
  and their sympathy for my way of doing things.

fields and sheep-grazing land adjacent to their houses or nearby. If they are lucky. When there is not enough land to raise a year's stock of corn and beans, the men and boys of a family will hire themselves out to work in the hot lowlands, either in the cornfields of other Indians, or in the coffee plantations of Mexicans. Family income can also be augmented by trade in produce, firewood, and charcoal, and by making goods for Indians in neighboring towns. Chamulas are the ingenious manufacturers of tables and chairs, harps and guitars, wool clothing, illegal liquor, and a whole range of simple household clay vessels.

Until recently, only a small number of families had permanent residence in the valley which contains the town's center—the municipal hall and the church, a government school and a clinic, a few stores. The great majority of people come to the center only for legal or religious business or when there is a fiesta or a market.

As a municipio, Chamula is nearly autonomous. The community court tries all sorts of cases except murders and land disputes with other towns. The president, elected to his three-year term, becomes the intermediary between his own place and the external forces which intend to have their effect on the town—the state government, and the national government working through the Instituto Nacional Indigenista (INI), a multipurpose program for the development of the Indian areas of Mexico.

In addition to the major elected officials, the town has a large group of officials appointed to one-year terms. These posts, called *cargos* in Spanish and *abtel* (meaning "work") in Tzotzil, are filled by people willing to give service or pressed into it because of their ability to bear the financial burden. There are also religious cargos, which involve a year's "care" for the figures of principal saints in the church, or the expense and energy for mounting the major religious festivals. Both civil and religious cargos give prestige to the people who serve them. Holders of cargos move to the center for a year in order to be near their work.

The religious system seems to be a coupling of pre-Conquest with Catholic beliefs and practices. Most babies are baptized by priests who visit during fiestas. The saints in the church have Spanish names and wan white faces. But the idea of the animal souls of a person which reside in the mountains, and flying spirits which inhabit the night, must come from an earlier and unrecorded time.

At the height of a fiesta, a visitor is impressed with the black and the white of 10,000 people dressed almost in uniform. Men normally wear white wool fringed *chamarras* (tunics) over cotton shirts and drawers. On a journey, a man carries his things in a leather or net bag with a shoulder strap and wears rubber tire-soled sandals. Men once plaited long bands of palm and had them sewn into tall conical, broad-brimmed hats, but now plastic-coated cowboy hats have come into fashion. Women and girls go barefoot. They dress in long black wool skirts secured with red waistbands and white cotton blouses under black shawls.

In 1963, Chamula was cool if not completely closed to outsiders. Tourists who bumped the ten miles up a dirt road in sagging taxis to see the big fiestas were tolerated for a morning, as long as they didn't try to take photographs in the church. Although a town law prohibiting regular residence by Ladinos (Spanish-speaking non-Indians) had been created in 1940 to get rid of tradesmen who cheated Indians, Ladinos working as teachers or doctors for INI were permitted to stay in the infirmary and the school in the center.

I was made nervous by casual warnings: the people in Chamula are *"bravo"*—tough or dangerous. The day before I was to go there, George Collier, then assistant director of the Harvard summer project, took me along on a visit to a lively old woman in a nearby town. She and George talked Tzotzil for a while. Then they discussed me in Spanish.

"And what's this one going to do?"

"I'm going to find him a place to live in Chamula."

The old lady looked me up and down. "So tall and fat," she said. She clucked her tongue and shook her head. "They'll kill him."

All three of us laughed.

My presence in Chamula was made possible by Eric Prokosch, an earlier student who had worked hard for two summers, first at convincing authorities it would be good for him to stay there, and then at making friends with people while he was studying in the center. George Collier made a plea for me before the President and set the conditions. I was a student; I wanted to learn the language and how things were done. Though I was tall, I wouldn't take up much room in a house and I could eat anything. I didn't need special food, just some beans and tortillas, and I wouldn't go walking around where I wasn't supposed to go.

The man whose family I came to live with, Mariano Hernández López, had his house in a paraje a forty-five-minute walk from the center. He was an *escribano* (an appointed scribe), and every day we went to the center and listened to the community court cases, or I accompanied him on town business. At noon we ate at the homes of other officials. Mariano took his job as my guide, or perhaps my guard, with great seriousness, teaching me what Tzotzil he could drum into my head, telling me stories, explaining my extraordinary presence to people as we walked home through the countryside. At night there were eight of us, including his wife and five children and the gringo, sleeping in an area about ten feet square under Mariano's high thatched roof. Mariano took me to ceremonies in which he performed and to fiestas in other towns. By moonlight we slid home drunk on precipitous slippery paths, carrying Mariano's sleeping younger children.

About once a week I would take the peso truck to San Cristóbal, have a bath and furiously pound out my notes. It was an involving time in my life.

There was never a question of whether I could submerge or lose myself in that scene. My height, and my clothes, my color and my halting ability with the language, all kept me apart. (Several years later, it was reported to me that they were saying a giant had once lived in Chamula.) But some people became a little accustomed to me. At the town court, a visitor would ask who I was, and an official would say, "Him? Oh, he's always just hanging around." Or, in the church while the officials under Mariano's tutelage were saying prayers and lighting candles for the advent of a fiesta, the person providing accompaniment would pass the guitar and tell me to keep up the playing because he was tired.

The next year, 1964, I returned for eight months' more study under somewhat different circumstances. Most of my time was spent in learning to interview in Tzotzil. With the help of anthropologist Gerald Williams, I acquired at least the ability to formulate reasonable questions and to record answers. My fieldnotes began to focus almost exclusively on the data necessary to build a description of ritual drinking events in Chamula, which was my part of a large group project.

What I had when I began the fieldwork were some of my senses—sight primarily, but also smell, taste, and touch. Spanish was an often poor second language not only for the people I lived with, but for me as well. Cut off and in a strange land, I watched as carefully as I could, and tried *not* to imagine I knew what people were thinking or feeling. I did not assume their dreams were like my own. (Later, thinking I knew more, in another work I dealt with beliefs and myths and dreams.) The rule I applied to what I could write was fairly stringent: when possible, record the manifestation of feeling, the action or the gesture, and not the interior state. Such a test of what you can know would eventually become debilitating, but I believe that for a beginner it is both honest and helpful.

Women play only a small part in *Crazy February*. Once I learned some Tzotzil I could talk and joke with older, married women, but it would have been considered suspect if I had asked to spend days sitting with women on hillsides watching sheep or at a waterhole washing clothes. Men in Chamula do not do such things. A man may know the shape of a woman's day from his own childhood, but it is a knowledge not easily available to a grown gringo.

✻   ✻   ✻   ✻   ✻   ✻

> "No, my reward will be seeing Chomtik in ten years, to see how it has changed."

The schoolmaster in *Crazy February* who looks to the future for his satisfaction means to play a significant part in bringing about the social changes he predicts. I have had the somewhat less well-deserved pleasure of revisiting Chamula at various times during ten years and of comparing the place as it is now with the one I wrote about.

In 1963 I observed a traditional peasant society which seemed extremely vulnerable to modernizing influences. The least sympathetic characters in the book are the ones who seek to disrupt an old order: either outsiders who work for change through the Indian Institute, without making any real attempt to figure out the existing genius and motive of the town, or Indians who have become enamored of the modern world and have somehow changed or corrupted or controverted themselves.

Chamula does seem to me to have changed in ten years, though not so drastically as the schoolmaster would have hoped. The signs are small but significant. When I was last there, the officials were helping replace a punctured tire on the used Volkswagen the town purchased for its President to drive to San Cristóbal on business. On the dirt road to the city is a large billboard which commands the drinking of Coca-Cola. There is some electricity in the center, brought by wires strung to poles erected in the plaza next to the large wooden crosses where the religious officials pray. A second floor has been added to the town hall, though not without a controversy. I was told that the President who proposed the addition levied a tax on every family. Then a time passed and there were no signs of construction and people became convinced the President had simply pocketed their money. And so one day five hundred men arrived in the center armed with their guns, intent either on deposing the President or, some say, on killing him. The matter was eventually settled and the second floor begun.

Writing today, I doubt that I would be as critical of the Indian Institute as I once was. Its announced goal—the complete integration of the Indian into the national social and economic life—has not been achieved yet. At least not in Chamula. But some of the Institute's programs have made people less vulnerable to exploitation. More men and women know Spanish well enough to make the language useful in trade. New roads and "cooperative" trucks allow people to get their produce to a larger variety of markets.

Finally, then, I find *Crazy February* poses a central important question: is it ever possible for a traditional society to maintain its values, or its integrity, in the face of powerful modernizing influences? The answer is still unclear to me. In spite of the superficial changes I have mentioned, ten years have proved the resilience of Chamula. True, if the recent discovery of oil in the area proves significant, or IBM de México suddenly decided Chamula was an ideal place for a transistor factory, then the place as I knew it might disappear overnight. But barring such extreme impositions, it seems that the way of life will continue its current flowering. That way may be intensely conservative, but over and over it demonstrates an adaptability which is the property only of living things.

*   *   *   *   *   *

People have wondered about the book's title. It comes from a speech composed for the annual fiesta of Carnaval by a man named Juan Pérez Jolote, which begins: "Chamulas! Crazy February! On this day, the twentieth of February, 1932, the first soldier came to Mexico, came to Guatemala, came to Tuxtla, came to Chiapa, came to San Cristóbal. He came here with flags, with drums, with trumpets. Viva!" In his autobiography, Juan Pérez Jolote says he does not know what his speech meant. It was given to him in a dream, perhaps by God.

Carnaval, which most often falls in February, is a fiesta of wildness, of men in women's clothing, mock battles with horse dung, and rituals run wrong on purpose. In the ancient Mayan calendar as it is recalled in Chamula, there are five especially evil days, and these also come in February.

For this paperback edition I have made a few minor word corrections in the text and have added a short glossary (*see* pp. 252-253).

May 1973   Carter Wilson
Santa Cruz

CRAZY FEBRUARY

Thirty thousand Indians live here. There must be thirty thousand warm places to sleep.

Why then would a man named Salvador and his son take to the paths around the mountains on an evening promising cold, and make a third come with them? They must be crazy, all of them. Everyone knows in the winter, in the spitting rain, the paths are red slick with mud. They must be crazy.

They are Mexicans and Indians. They live here in the mountains of their own free will. Filthy, dumb, eying progress suspiciously as if it were some buzzard in the sky.

Well, let the crazy man Salvador come to the village. Let him find his own dry place to sleep away from home. Don't disturb him. Don't even ask him why he came.

PART ONE:

THE PRESIDENT

1   The Man Salvador

RAIN BEGAN JUST AS the three men reached the top of the last hill before the village. It came down soft, barely touching the brims of their hats, barely rustling the needles on the pine trees. The first man did not look down into the valley, he went on. The second had the burden and was breathing hard between his closed and clenched teeth. He was cold. Behind him he could hear the third, waiting for him to start the descent.

The third waited. From the gap in the hill he could see the whole valley, though clouds made it dark and hid the moon.

The moon was there, to his left, only a lightened gray blur behind the clouds. He could see the church, it was white. And the long government building, also white. The houses on the hills, black. The two roads to the plaza, yes. And the big crosses. He could make out one of them—on a hill to his right—but the others were hidden in the dark.

The first two men were well along now. They had dropped below him and were out of sight. The wind drove the rain, it got under his hat to the back of his neck, so he hunched his shoulders and went on. He heard his father slip once in the mud. Then he heard the second man's burden as it slammed against a rock, a shuddering sound. He caught up with them as they were picking their way between the boulders, using their hands to steady themselves. The load on the second man's back swayed and rolled each time he took a step.

When he reached the bottom of the hill, the first man rested. But as soon as the other two caught up with him, he set out again, taking longer strides now that he was on an open road. They began passing houses, closed and dark. Inside they could hear a woman asking who was going by, but she received no answer. Finally one door opened and a boy's head showed in the crack of light. Then the door was closed and bolted from the inside. The three continued walking, heads bent against the rain.

Before one dead house the first man stopped.

"Do you want to warm your heart, boy?" he called out.

The second man didn't answer, but the third did. "Yes, Father."

The first man stepped closer to the dead house. "Uncle, I've come," he called, looking away from the door.

"You've come." It was an old woman's voice that answered, high and cracked.

"Do you have *posh*?" the father asked.

There was silence from the house. The wind whistled around and in a pen nearby the sheep moved closer together for warmth.

"Where are you from?" It was a man's voice now.

"From Cruztik. I'm Salvador."

The door opened, creaking. A man stood in the light. "Where are you going?"

Still the father did not look at the door. "I have business with the President," he mumbled, barely opening his mouth.

The other man recognized him. "I have some strong *posh*. Come in." He swung open the door and stepped back. The father and son went inside where it was warmer.

"A lot of cold," said the father. Then he explained about the boy they had brought with the load, and the other man and his wife nodded. The woman turned away.

"No, I don't want him in the house. You're right. There's room to sit close under the roof where the rain doesn't come." The other man went to the doorway, curious, and looked hard at the boy and his burden before telling him he could sit under the eaves.

Those inside agreed to leave the door open a bit so they could watch the boy outside. There was little danger he would get away, said the man Salvador. They had lashed his load to him with ropes.

The old woman went to the back of the room and sat beside the altar, near where her children were sleeping.

As she poured liquor from the big jug to a bottle she could hear this Salvador telling the story over again. A hard one to believe. She could hear the wind from the doorway blowing on the fire. It would die down soon with wind like that, so she brought some more wood when she brought the liquor.

She gave the bottle to the younger of the two visitors. He poured a full glass for her husband. At least these people from far away knew the right thing to do, though they were strange with their long hair and glazed eyes. People from that part, from Cruztik, were wild and strange. She wondered if they were telling the truth about the boy outside under the eaves. Maybe they had done it themselves.

She kneeled and sat heavily on her feet and stirred her fire. She was tired, she hoped they would go soon so she could sleep. Her husband drank, then the man Salvador. Then her husband poured for the boy. When he got the bottle back the son gave her a glass. She thanked the man Salvador and turned away to drink. The stuff was strong and burned her inside and made her eyes smart the way smoke from the fire did. She should have added more water to the jug. Her husband would tell her that when the strangers left.

The son took a glass outside and they could hear the other boy murmur something. His burden hit against the side of the house, making the rafters crack.

"He's there?" asked the father when the son returned.

"He was asleep."

They finished the bottle, and then Salvador asked for a half more, which the wife brought. They did not talk much, these strangers. They looked dazed at the fire except when they were drinking. Their clothes were dirty

and their legs were caked with mud. Neither had even
sandals.

"Thank you, Uncle," Salvador said, getting up from his
stool and fishing for something under his tunic. He brought
out a red handkerchief, tied tight. After picking nervously
at the knots he got it open and gave two peso pieces to the
man of the house.

"When you finish your business with the President,"
said the other man, "you and your son can sleep here, for
the night."

"No," said Salvador, "we'll go to my sister's husband,
thank you." He put on his hat. The son was lingering by
the fire, warming his hands.

"Who is your sister?" the man of the house asked quietly, pretending he didn't care.

"The new wife of Juan López Oso." The man Salvador
seemed proud.

The woman did not speak. She did not know that Juan
López Oso had a new wife. But she knew he had not been
seen in the village for several weeks, and that his store
was closed. However, this was none of her business.

"Uncle, would you tell me where is the President's
house?"

"There behind the big house of the Doctor."

Salvador nodded.

"You know the path?"

"Yes, thank you. We're going."

"Go on, then."

Outside the wind was gone. They woke the boy and
helped him stagger to his feet.

The little procession turned off the road before reaching
the Doctor's house. Gaslights were on inside the Doctor's
and cast beams of yellow onto the path. The President's

house must be the big one with a tile roof and mud-brick walls. Lean dogs outside growled and then began to yelp when the three came to the front yard. They stood outside and listened. At first the house seemed as dead as all the others. Then they heard voices, talking Spanish. They did not know who might be inside, or what was being said. Finally music and men singing—

> *Jalisco, Jalisco is my beloved home*
> *And I will never roam again. . . .*

Although the men outside in the cold could not understand the words, they recognized this as music from either a radio or a record player.

The man Salvador did not know how to call, what he might be interrupting. He thought of his long evening's trip through the mountains, how he had done his duty and would now lose a day's work for it. He thought the President too had a duty, but he didn't call out.

"It's so cold," murmured the boy behind him. It was not his son, but the boy with the load. So Salvador called.

"President!"

The music inside stopped.

"I have a man here, President."

Someone stirred inside and coughed. The door cracked and the owlish head of the President appeared. He looked around, up at the night sky.

"What's going on?" he asked, holding the phlegm in his mouth.

"I have a dead man here, President."

The President came outside, both hands inside his tunic. He peered into the dark and then spat the phlegm on the ground. The dogs were silent now, sniffing at the strangers.

The President expected to know the man when he said

he was from Cruztik. The President had been school-teacher in that hamlet for three years, and he knew most of the men from there.

But the face of the man who had spoken was old and wrinkled. He did not know it. The second man, young, was bent over, supporting the weight of the body.

"Maestro!" called the third, smiling when he recognized his old teacher. The boy bowed and the President touched him on the head, releasing him.

No one knew how he still enjoyed being called "Maestro." In his own mind the title fitted his idea of himself much better than "President."

"Do you know the name of this dead man?" asked the President.

All of the men in a tiny hamlet like Cruztik knew each other. But when they had killed one of their neighbors the man who had courage enough to bring the body to the village pretended to have no idea who the dead one could be. The neighbor would say he had only been coming home and crossing the road found the body of a stranger in a ditch.

The President sighed, feeling the thickness of his chest. He had heard this story a hundred times.

However, the man Salvador said he knew the murdered man. It was his wife's brother, and Salvador gave the name. He was killed last night in a fight.

"How?"

"With a whip and a machete."

The President went to see. They had strapped two poles to the back of a chair, the body was lashed tightly to the chair, and the chair tied to the carrier's back.

The dead man sat upright, his arms at his sides as though he were at attention, his legs crossed and pushing against his chest. His head was thrown back and he seemed to be squinting at the clouds, smiling in some grim pleasure. There were dark scars of clotted blood across his forehead, and rusty blood in his thin white hair.

The carrier faltered as the President watched. The dead man's head bobbed.

"You don't know how it happened?"

"Yes. He fought with his son and his son killed him. Last night. We would have brought him earlier, but I had to burn my cornfield today."

The President nodded, understanding. "And the boy, the man's son?" he asked.

"This is the boy," Salvador said.

The President was surprised. He expected the son would have gotten away, would already be halfway down the mountains toward hot country, where he might find anonymity and work on the coffee fincas.

The President bent down to see the boy's face. He was shocked by few things these days, but the idea of a boy killing his father was colder than the rain. The boy's head was tilted down and the President seized his black hair and yanked up the head. But he didn't look. The boy had a right to be alone with his shame, if he had it.

Salvador asked what the President would do.

"Tonight they will both be put in the jail, tomorrow the Doctor will cut the old man and they will bury him and the next day the boy—we will take the boy to San Martín."

"To the prison?" Salvador asked, although he already knew the answer. The prison called Santo Domingo stood next to the market in San Martín and soldiers patrolled the yard in brown uniforms, carrying guns. Bad Indians— killers and thieves—were put there.

"No," said the President, "first there will be a trial in town. You will have to be there."

The President left Salvador to think about this and went into his house. His wife was sitting by the fire and his eldest son, Eliseo, was leaning close to the radio. When his father asked him, Eliseo took the heavy key ring, put on his Mexican jacket, and went out to take the dead man and the killer to jail.

Eliseo was young, eighteen, and the idea of murder and the duty given him made him self-important. He ordered the boy to come quickly, since Eliseo didn't like standing in the cold. Passing the Doctor's lighted windows he caught a look at the other boy's face. The boy was younger. Out in the plaza Eliseo stopped and told the other to wait. He ran through the mud to the store of his friend Jacinto, rapped on the door, and called in Spanish.

"Come on, Jacinto, we're going to put a dead man and a killer in jail."

A higher voice answered from the back of the store. "Go away, Eliseo, you're drunk."

Eliseo wasn't drunk, but he could tell from the voice that his friend had been drinking. "Come on." He was impatient.

"But Eliseo, I'm getting my woman again. The second time tonight. Go away please. Sleep at your father's house tonight. I'm screwing my wife!" Inside Jacinto pounded the table before him several times. His wife looked up from the bed where she was sitting nursing her baby.

Eliseo grinned and pushed with his shoulder against the door. Jacinto leaped up and began pushing back from inside.

"You aren't getting her!" Eliseo cried in Spanish.

"Find your own wife. Don't bother me, Eliseo! Ho, you're breaking down the door!"

"Then come on!"

A moment later Jacinto came outside, pulling on a jacket. "And don't stop me any more when I'm getting my woman." He pretended anger, and then his moon face broke out in a smile. Eliseo told him the story as they returned to the place where the boy was waiting.

The killer had fallen to his knees.

"Ho!" Jacinto yelled when they came up. He kicked at the boy and inspected the body. "Why did you do it?"

The boy got to his feet without giving any answer. He kept his head down as they walked across the plaza. The boy didn't look up as they passed the church with its huge white façade, but when they got to the front of the government building he could see the dark square hole in the wall which was the jail, and he stopped.

"Come on," Jacinto ordered, using all of his solid little strength to throw another kick at the boy. The burden shuddered and the body's head nodded.

Eliseo was ahead of them, rattling the big keys in the double lock. The door of heavy latticed beams swung open and they met a damp smell of straw. Jacinto pulled at the boy's arm. "Go on, the rats are hungry."

"Are there rats?" asked the boy softly.

"Rats? They'll eat your father before morning and then you." Jacinto laughed, winking at Eliseo. Eliseo laughed too and watched the fear grow on the boy's dumb face.

Jacinto pushed again.

The boy resisted, staring into the dark. Then he gave up and was shoved into the cell where he fell on top of the body.

Eliseo swung the door shut and began locking it. Inside the boy was crying. He rolled over the body and tried to stand again.

"Jacinto?"

"What?"

"Go take it off his back."

"No, not me. I'm not going in there." Jacinto danced around behind his friend.

Eliseo unlocked the door again and went inside. Since he couldn't see in the dark, he found the boy by following the crying sound. They had lashed the father and son together at the waist, the ropes were tied on the father's chest, where the son couldn't reach them. Recklessly and quickly Eliseo turned the body and began to untie the knots. Underneath the boy writhed, trying to get loose. He swept his arms helplessly through the straw, grabbing fistfuls.

Eliseo was sweating when he finally got the two disconnected. The boy sighed and whimpered, freed himself of his father and then lay still on the floor.

When Eliseo came out, Jacinto hung on the wooden bars and shouted into the hollow dark, "The Doctor will open his head, cut it off, open him inside! You'll see that!"

The two free boys, in high spirits, raced each other back across the silent plaza. His father's key ring slapped against Eliseo's side. They went to Jacinto's store. Each ran for it, aware now the excitement was over how cold it really was.

"Do you know how to drink brandy?" Jacinto asked as they crashed, panting, into the store.

"I'll pay!" said Eliseo.

Jacinto found the bottle he had brought from San Martín in the afternoon. "Cigarettes too."

The President waited in his house, expecting Eliseo would return to listen to the radio some more. As he waited, the President wondered why any boy would kill his father. It was incomprehensible to him, and the President had little patience with strange ideas. He could not imagine Eliseo, even when drunk, coming at him with a whip or a machete. They never disagreed. If the boy didn't like what his father told him, he would grow silent and stare into the fire. Or leap up and go off to see his friend Jacinto and to drink. Of course it might be different if they still lived in Cruztik where nothing ever happened. Or if they didn't have enough money. Or even if Eliseo lived at home, instead of in Jacinto's store.

The President wondered if he had taught the killer. He hadn't recalled the name when the man Salvador said it, and thought not. He wished he had been more curious and had looked into the boy's face to find out. But he would know in the morning, he would have to look at that face many times in the next few days.

The man Salvador was still standing under the eaves of the house, so the President got up and went to the door. "You don't have to stay."

Salvador seemed to have been dozing. Now he shook himself awake. "President," he said, "pardon me. I have a favor to ask you."

"What is it?"

Salvador carried a leather bag at his side. From it he pulled a large bottle of liquor. "President," he said, "will you take this little bottle of *posh* as a gift?"

"I don't drink," said the President. But he invited the man Salvador inside and put him in a chair close to the fire. The radio was crackling with static and the President turned it off before he himself sat down.

Salvador talked quickly in a high, nervous voice, turning the refused bottle in his hand. "President, your scribes came to tell me I have to serve as First Gobernador from my place in Cruztik this year."

The President coughed and spat on the floor. He knew what the man wanted.

"I—President, I can't serve this year. I'm not a rich man, like my neighbors say. I'm not as rich as they are. I can't afford to live here for a full year in the village, I can't pay the prices an official pays. My wife is sick now. I was here before, I was an Alcalde from Cruztik just seven years ago, my little son died when I was here—"

Salvador had been thinking of his story all during the two-hour walk from his home. He talked very fast now, faster than he could remember talking before. His son stood behind him at the door.

"President, I brought in the killer, the body, all of it. I lost a day of work, a day of my son's work. I'm not a rich man like some. I won't be able to work tomorrow. Isn't that enough? I brought him—"

The President, bored and almost angry, interrupted the other man. "Isn't that enough? What's enough? I was made President two years ago! Did I try to get out of it? I taught school before that, I made my money from the Indian Institute. But I was President for one year as the others had been, because they asked me to be President. The others served one year, then went home. They asked me to serve another year, then another. I'm doing it. You spend two days, but what about three years?"

"But President, I'm a poor man, my wife is sick—"

"Be quiet. What about me? I'm a poor man too. My wife *died*."

Salvador looked around the room. The radio there. He did not know what it cost, but it came from San Martín, and only the rich store owners in the village had them. The President's new wife by the fire had a black wool skirt that looked new, and plenty of embroidery on her blouse. Salvador knew what these things were worth. A dark wood guitar leaned against one chair. Not like Indian guitars, it must be from town. The President had a gold watch on his wrist. Watches cost over two hundred pesos. There was a tile roof on the President's house. Salvador did not believe the President, but he could not say so.

The President smiled and coughed, his anger gone. He was tired and wanted to be rid of this Salvador. "Do you have a place to sleep tonight? You can stay on the porch of the government building, the Cabildo."

"Thank you, President. We'll go to the house of my sister's new husband."

"What's his name?"

"Juan López Oso."

The President laughed. The people from the hamlets never knew anything. "He hasn't been here in the village for three weeks."

"Well," Salvador said, "I'll go to see."

So the President told the man from Cruztik where Juan López Oso lived, and in return accepted the liquor when Salvador offered it again. The President could give the *posh* to Eliseo, or sell it somewhere.

Salvador and his son went outside, passed the Doctor's house, dark now, and went to the big open plaza. There was talking behind the door of the best store, but silence elsewhere. They called in front of the store of Juan López Oso, but got no reply, so they returned to the house of the man who sold them liquor and crept onto the porch. There were no dogs to warn the people inside that they had come, and no one stirred. The son took out a pile of tortillas wrapped in a handkerchief, and gave half to his father. By the time they had finished the clouds began to break up. The moon was in the west, white and wet, and it looked as though she were chasing the clouds away from her.

The President slept well at first, waking only to cough and clear his throat. Half asleep he could see Cruztik, the schoolhouse in the cleft between the two mountains, the river and the pool where he made the boys wash in the morning. The old bus which ran in from the village of San Ramón in the morning, ground past the school and disappeared out of the valley on the way to San Martín. He could hear the corn at night in the high wind, the sudden crack as stalks broke. He remembered leading an excited group of the schoolboys through the hills once to the village for the fiesta at Carnaval. And getting to the village to be told his wife had died. They got him drunk and took him back to Cruztik, and there was no school for a month while he tried to dispel his sadness with cheap brandy. He could still taste the loneliness and the idea he had been wrong to leave his wife alone so long while he taught in Cruztik. He tasted these things though his new woman breathed heavily beside him and his new baby son slept curled against his chest. With the loneliness he could not sleep and waited quietly until it grew light and the woman got up and went outside to fetch water.

2 Doctor Méndez

THE DOCTOR FIRST heard of the murder and the body when his assistant Mario came to work in the morning.

Mario strode through the big empty waiting room

where the sun poured in and columns of dust slanted up to the windows. It was intensely quiet there, and colder than outside. Mario started charcoal burning in the kitchen.

The Doctor got up and smoked his first cigarette of the day while he dressed, then went to the kitchen. Mario had washed before he came to work, his hair was combed wet and a drop of water still hung from his chin. After Mario put on water for coffee and laid out three eggs for the Doctor to cook, the Doctor gave him a peso to go buy tortillas from the Secretary's wife. Mario looked at his watch, and told the Doctor the bad news about the murder, smiling.

The Doctor wondered if Mario was pleased with the prospect of an autopsy. The assistant seemed to get some malignant pleasure out of the work whenever they performed an autopsy together. But he was probably as disgusted with the possibility as the Doctor. After all, Mario did not like filth and stench either.

It was for this reason the Doctor had chosen Mario as his assistant. A lot of these Indians spoke decent enough Spanish. Plenty of them were willing to make the good money. But Mario was wearing a clean white wool tunic and clean shirt the day the Doctor had to make his choice, and since Mario had this instinct, Méndez had worked hard in the succeeding months to cultivate it.

The Doctor was duly proud of the result. Changing a man's habit of life was like skin grafting. You used all your skill for a tiny piece of work, and sometimes nature or the body fought against you. The graft would not take. But if the body was willing, you could almost see the growth from the moment you first laid the patch in place.

Having learned cleanliness and order, Mario was proceeding to learn sanity. The Doctor had explained to him how the Indian liquor would eventually rot him inside, and to the Doctor's knowledge Mario no longer drank *posh*. Instead the assistant had taken to brandy, which he drank with the Doctor, or from his own supply he brought from town.

At times the Doctor worried. What would Mario do with his new expensive taste when the Doctor's year was up and he went away? The new doctor would choose his own assistant. But that was not Méndez's current problem. Besides, he saw in Mario an innate ability to get along. The boy's self-confidence, his ready smile, all of these things which the Doctor admired would stand him in good stead for the rest of his life.

Mario returned with the pile of white tortillas and the Doctor himself made the coffee and fixed the eggs. While doing so, he replanned his day. Originally he had thought to spend the day in San Martín with his mistress. Now the autopsy intervened. It would take the morning and perhaps part of the afternoon. Well, he could still make the truck to town at two o'clock. His woman would be angry, but he had no control over circumstances. She had no cause for anger. If she had any strength of character she would have come to the village to live with him long ago.

Someone knocked on the front door, and Mario padded away to answer it. He returned with the Maestro from the school. The Doctor did not especially like this man, but since they were thrown together in the village, the Doctor was determined to be friendly.

The Maestro was a short boy, barely in his twenties. He combed his hair carefully into a pompadour which made his face even squarer. The smile was big and open, so you had to look at the close, squinty eyes to find out what the Maestro was really like. Watching the eyes you could tell the smile was usually cruel. The Maestro had been here longer—two years—he knew the Indian language, and the Indian officials had respect for him. The Doctor would watch from his infirmary window as the Maestro walked jauntily to the government building with some request. And the Maestro would get it, because he pretended to speak their language. He was quick and decisive in his actions, the Maestro, and he moved with energy. The Doctor would watch again later in the day when the Maestro led the school children out to march around the plaza. Then the Maestro cracked orders, blew his whistle and stepped out lively in front of the ragged children. Finally the Doctor would have his laugh for the day. A child Moses with his army, a silly, immature puppet.

"What's the matter? You smell food all the way from the schoolhouse?" he asked the Maestro while he cracked the eggs into the frying pan.

"No, the Secretary's wife told me you got all the fresh tortillas."

"Oh. You want some?"

"Thank you. Actually, I'm hungry this morning. The cold up here makes me hungry."

"Well then, why don't you stay and eat with Mario and myself?"

The Doctor tried to act hearty and friendly, but the effort failed.

The Maestro knew where he stood in the Doctor's eyes. Maybe they both worked for the Indian Institute, and made the same salary. But the Doctor considered himself to be a thousand times better. He had a full University education, he was older, he came from a good family in the north (so they said), and at the end of his year he would find a lucrative practice in Mexico City or in Guadalajara. The Maestro, on the other hand, was the child of the Indian Institute. They taught him, they made him the head of the six Chomtik schools. Some day they might give him a good administrative job in San Martín. Then at the end of his life he might be sent to Mexico City, to sit at a desk in the Institute headquarters. The future had possibilities for the Maestro, but he knew he had no reason to try to read the future the Institute had given him.

He sat down at the Doctor's table, took one of the tortillas, ripped it in two and stuffed a half into his mouth. Méndez thought he had bad manners, so why not give him reason to think so.

"Did you see the latest *Siempre*?" the Maestro asked.

"Yes," said the Doctor, stirring his eggs. "I have it in there in my room." *Siempre*, he thought, was the magazine for the intellectuals. He wondered what the Maestro could get out of it.

"They have a drawing this week, of Uncle Sam in a ricksha being pulled by Latin America, and Castro going by on a motorbike. Uncle Sam is saying, 'Why do you want a motorbike when we've already got automobiles?' That's pretty good." The Maestro laughed sharply.

The Doctor had been amused by the cartoon, but would not admit it to the Maestro. He held the upper hand in this, too. He knew some English and the Maestro knew none. In their arguments, therefore, he defended the United States. Not because the United States wasn't wrong, but because it was juvenile and unhistoric of the Maestro to trot out his little socialist-nationalist banner every time the Great One to the North was mentioned.

He served the eggs, equal portions for all. Mario poured the coffee and sat down. The Indian was obviously hungry, and the Doctor enjoyed watching his boy eat so well. He ate rapidly himself, at first. Then he told the Maestro about the killing and the body he would have to dissect.

"Good practice for you."

The Doctor agreed it was. How could he explain to the layman that it was no practice at all? It was a butchery done as fast as possible before the stench overcame you. It was a government formality from which he could learn nothing. "It's unedifying work, though," he admitted.

"All of your work here must be unedifying. At the school we are at least teaching them something useful. The children leave us with Spanish and a skill, to confront the world outside. All you can do is tell the government in San Martín what one man died of, something we already know. And give medicine to one or two a day, so they won't die this time, at least. Pretty hopeless for you."

The Doctor shrugged and took up his coffee. The steam rose into his mustache and made his lips warm, as though he had been kissed.

What the Maestro had said was true, he thought, but it was no revelation to him. It was a summation of the reasons he hated the place. The Indians would not come to him, he could not go to them, so he waited out his year in the infirmary. He read medical books, all the cures for the diseases he knew they carried. When he was drunk he begged Mario to bring him the sick people, but Mario never made good his promises.

"Do you think *your* work does any good? Really?" asked the Doctor.

The Maestro looked up quickly, and then at Mario.

The Maestro trusts no one, thought the Doctor. How can he teach Indians when he doesn't trust them?

Mario took the plates away and went outside to get water to wash them.

"Of course my work does good. These people learn slowly, that's all. You, Doctor, have no idea of what time is here. You spend your one year, and then you'll go away. But the Institute's work in education doesn't end when your year is up."

"And you're going to change these people, bring them progress?"

"Certainly." All of the Maestro's energy was forced into one word.

"One Language for All Mexico? One Way of Life?"

The Maestro stood up. "No, I don't believe the slogans either. They are for the people and the politicians."

The Doctor had always hated the idealists who thought they were too practical to believe in ideals.

"So what's in it for you?" Méndez asked. "The money?" He laughed.

The Maestro would have liked to admit that the money was important to him, but he could not. "No, my reward will be seeing Chomtik in ten years, to see how it has changed."

The Doctor even disliked the little part of himself which he classified as idealist. That part of him made him choose the village in the mountains when he got out of medical school. That part of him was blind to what everyone said, that part of him would never admit that one man can't change the world. That part admired the Maestro and his patience.

"And in ten years the big guns of the National Government will come to see Chomtik again. And the Institute will erect another sign on the road: 'Chomtik, This Village the Labor of the National Indian Institute.' And the same Indians who tore down the first sign will come again with their axes and tear it down again."

The Maestro remained silent. He did not want to fight with the Doctor. Somehow he always came out the worse in their arguments. There was some unfair advantage for the Doctor. His education was almost like his height would be in a real fight.

Mario returned with the pail of water and cleared the table. The Doctor offered the Maestro a drink of brandy and a cigarette, thinking that for once he had opened the rift between them too wide.

"No, the Institute is sending out an official from Mexico City this morning to inspect the place. I have to be sober when he comes."

As though he hadn't heard, the Doctor took down the bottle and got out glasses.

"Just a little one for the cold," he said. "We won't get drunk. This is good stuff."

He thought of the Institute officials. The fat men with little pencil mustaches, accompanied by their wives, the gray carbon look of the Mexico City office still on them. They would wonder why there were no Indians in the infirmary that morning. With their suspicious little minds and eyes in full function, they tried to see everything. And often they succeeded.

The body became the excuse. The Doctor could see himself shaking his big black mane sadly, full of infinite pity for the Indians in their drunkenness. Yes, sir, he was killed at a drunken fight. By his own son. Yes, the effects of alcoholism. There is little the Institute can do, but we try. No, it happens rarely, rarely. Yes, a terrible thing. Terrible. Do you want to see the body? No, it's not very pleasant. Well then, come have a look, but I wouldn't bring your wife or your daughter. Not for the ladies with the weak stomachs.

When the Doctor poured three glasses the Maestro seemed surprised. What did the Maestro expect him to do, leave out Mario? The difference between men who are egalitarian in their hearts and those who are egalitarian in their speech. Or maybe the difference between the man of good background and the man who has climbed up from poverty. The Doctor knew nothing of the Maestro's background, and preferred to leave it that way, all conjecture.

"That's good brandy," the Maestro admitted.

"Here, there's only a little left, take it," said Méndez.

"No, I have to go."

Maybe youth's impatience, thought the Doctor. Maybe just bad manners. Or a calculation. The Maestro leaves everything unfinished. He tells you how he has enjoyed your brandy, but he does not finish his glass. When he makes love he probably leaves the girl hungry, and himself hungry too.

There was a woman teacher named Carla at the school, fat, with a low forehead and thick hair. The Doctor was sure the Maestro was sleeping with her there in the teachers' house. The other male teacher had said as much, and Mario giggled, confirming it, when the Doctor asked him. Well, good for the Maestro, excellent for the girl. The Doctor had checked his jealousy long ago as unworthy. Now he only wanted to share the secret with someone to whom it would matter. His own woman in town wouldn't care.

At the front door the Doctor stopped. "And how's Carla?"

The Maestro looked out across the plaza to the school. The sun was bright and the children were arriving by twos and threes. At the basketball court a game had begun. "She's well."

"You didn't share her bed and board this morning?"

"No, she was late getting up and didn't make breakfast for us. Here, it's nine o'clock. Thank you for the food and the cigarette." The Maestro went out into the sunlight. A moment later the Doctor could hear him blow his whistle and start cracking orders to the older children.

Thanks for the food. Thanks for the cigarette. But not for the brandy. The Maestro showed he hadn't really wanted that. No, she didn't make breakfast for us. For us, the schoolteachers. We have a happy communal life over there, away from you. You aren't invited. And I'm not telling you about Carla and myself. Think what you want to think.

The Doctor went to his bedroom and selected a large orange from the row he was hoarding on the bookcase under his window. Mario brought his pail and began the slow work of mopping the waiting room floor.

"Are we going to open it this morning?" Mario asked.

"No. We have the autopsy."

Mario giggled.

The Doctor went out on the front porch, eating his orange. A little group of Indian men and women were walking across the plaza. The two men in front carried native guitars and were strumming that eternal tune to the patron saint of Chomtik. Then came a man, obviously old, helped by a boy. Behind them a man in a black tunic with a tall package of candles in his leather bag. The candles were wrapped in paper which had colored flowers on the outside. Last, two women, their wool shawls pulled up around their faces.

"Mario, come here."

Mario came to the door.

"What are those people doing there? Those going to the church."

"They're going to pray to the saints."

"That man in the black tunic—is he a curer?"

"Which one?"

The Doctor was irritated. There was only one man in a black tunic. The Doctor pointed. "There. Is he a curer?"

"What curer?"

"Is that man a doctor?"

"No." Mario risked a smile. "You are the doctor here in Chomtik." He returned to his pail and mop, and the Doctor could hear him giggling to himself.

So the barrier was still there, the Doctor thought. Mario was his friend in everything. They shared experiences, they shared bottles. The Doctor shared in Mario's life. But still he wouldn't tell about the curers. Perhaps there weren't as many as the people at the Institute said there were. Mario was now an enlightened young man, he knew what medicine, real medicine, did. Probably he just didn't want the Doctor to know how stupid his people could be. The way the Maestro didn't want the Indian to know how little some Mexicans valued the education he dealt out every day. Well, thought the Doctor, a little secrecy is every man's prerogative.

The group of worshipers prayed in front of the church, looking across the valley to the big double cross of San Pedro on its own hill behind the government building. The yellow arch of the doorway framed them.

The only time an Indian looks up from his feet, thought the Doctor, is when he prays to his God. Then he builds his God a house seven or eight times higher than an Indian's house, with an arch three times a man's height. But the Indian seals up the entrance with a board wall painted blue. He stumbles into the dark of the church through a door barely big enough for a standing boy. That grand arch, sealed up. The Doctor thought there was some analogy to be made, but he did not trace it. He thought all Mexicans who made beautiful pronouncements about the Indians were foolish. Sentimental. The Indians were men and they suffered like everyone else. He saw their suffering close up, and it was not beautiful or pure. Indians died like everyone else, he said. They were a little tougher, that was true, but they were also dirty and more stupid. That was also true. The intellectuals in Mexico City could fawn over the Indian, but the Doctor didn't see any intellectuals in the plaza of Chomtik that morning. None of them would help him wash the instruments after the autopsy.

The President hobbled out into the plaza on his way to the government building. He wore thick sandals with rubber soles, but looked as though every step on the mud clods was painful. He eyed the sun like some old night creature forced into the daylight. A lizard, the Doctor thought, as he hailed the President and explained he would come for the body later. The President stopped to chat, but then found nothing to say to Méndez.

Because of the wool tunics, hanging knee-length and belted at the waist, and because the men kept their hands inside at the chest, it was hard to tell about their strength and girth. But he could tell from the President's face and his legs that the man was thin. Thinner than when the

Doctor arrived. The answer, of course, could be heard. The President coughed and cleared his throat, a rasping harsh sound like the engine in an old car. Then he spat on the ground and inspected his phlegm.

The Doctor knew he had tuberculosis. He had said so in a report to the Institute Director in San Martín. But the almighties at the Institute station in town never replied. If it was unimportant to them that the President would die soon, the Doctor found it unimportant to himself. He hoped no one would demand an autopsy. He thought well enough of the President. The President had some learning and more dignity than any of the other Indians. At times he could be funny. The Doctor didn't want the unpleasant duty of cutting up such a man.

Having nothing to say, the President left for the Cabildo. The last of the school children came into the plaza and raced each other to the classroom. The Doctor admired their energy. As the President walked his uncomfortable way across the plaza he seemed to have strings attached to him, for as he went other old men appeared behind him and on either side. They came singly, and then joined in pairs. By the time the President got to the government building, ten or twelve old men, also in white tunics and broad-brimmed hats, were on their way to join him. They too seemed to protest every step.

The Doctor told himself that there were many more remote, deadly places he could have secreted himself for a year. At least things sometimes happened in Chomtik, if you waited long enough, and had the patience to watch. There were some places in Mexico, he knew, where events hung for days like a drop of water on the tap.

He turned to the idea of the autopsy. It filled the morn-

ing for him, it might take part of the afternoon. If he
didn't get the truck until two, he would not be in San
Martín before three. That would make the evening in bed
with his woman more precious.

3   The President

THE PRESIDENT WANDERED
onto the porch of the Cabildo. He was tempted to go
down to the other end and have a look at the killer, but
he put this off.

The office was empty, except for the red and green
chairs, the oilcloth-covered tables, the paraphernalia of
the village Secretary, Don Concepción—carbon paper,
typewriter, reports. From their frames the great men of
Mexico stared down at the President. Hidalgo, Juárez,
Díaz, Cárdenas, López Mateos and the others. He went
and looked again at the photograph of López Mateos, the
only one of these men he knew.

They had met that great fiesta day the National President came to visit the village. López Mateos had given the
President his big beefy hand and said, "So you are a
President too. It's hard work, isn't it?" Everyone laughed.
Then López Mateos had said, "I like your village." A polite thing to say, nothing more. But it had struck the President. For the moment he felt that this was his village, and
whatever came of it was his work.

Don Concepción came in from his house next door, talking to himself. The Secretary was old, bald, squat and
flabby, his face was a brown Saint Bernard's with four or
five folds of chin, and he looked out at the world over

rimless and useless spectacles. He wasn't an Indian but he could speak Tzotzil, the Indian language, in a graveled, halting voice. He typed the village's correspondence with painful slowness, and he was respectful to the President as he said good morning.

Don Concepción totally lacked ambition and had whiled away his eighteen years of servitude by planting eighteen babies, one a year, in the belly of his half-Indian wife. Many of the offspring still lived with their father in his house behind the government building.

The President told Don Concepción about the murder and the surprising fact that the murderer was the man's son. Then he took out a cigarette, and Don Concepción asked if he might borrow one. The President did not usually give away his cigarettes as other Indians did, but he sometimes lent them to Don Concepción.

The old clock on the wall with its weights and ornate face beat away the minutes. The President sucked the smoke of his cigarette. Outside he could hear the officials who had come for the morning's work. They talked among themselves, joking a little, but when he came outside they grew quiet.

He knew them, but still they fell silent before him. After a month they did not know what he thought. Just as well. These men were not his companions, they touched his life only at the edges. At the end of the year, in December, they would begin packing up their households in the village, their sons would come to help take their possessions home. Then at the New Year each of them would get drunk for a last time, and early some morning disappear, back to his hamlet. After the proper ceremonies a new sea of old faces would appear, and take on the names of the ones who disappeared. Gobernador, Alcalde, Síndico.

There were sixty titles for the President to attach to new men. He found it more difficult to do each year.

Though it was early there were people waiting for him, so the President went to the cement bench in the courtyard. He sat in the middle and the officials shook his hand, one light pass, before each took his seat on the bench. Some tilted the brims of their hats down to keep out the sun.

An old woman sat waiting in the courtyard, pulling her shawl tight around her face. A young girl with a crying baby sat beside the woman. Near them, but separate, was a group of men and their own wives.

The old woman, unsure of herself, got up, came to the President and knelt before him. The girl with the baby followed. The President gave his hand for the woman to touch, and then rested his hand briefly on the girl's bowed head.

The old woman began, begging pardon for bothering the President, but her daughter (she barely indicated the girl with a turn of her head) had been wronged by her husband, after only a year of marriage.

The President sighed and threw his cigarette out on the grass. He knew all that would happen, but he had to ask where the husband was. The old woman nodded toward the group of men. The President called them and they came. The men touched the President's hand, touched the hands of the other officials, bowing to the oldest. They were as embarrassed and uncomfortable as the old woman. People from the hamlets were always uneasy when they brought cases to the President. These had been walking since daybreak, two silent groups, neither speaking to the other on the path. But now in the village, before the eminence of the President, they did not show their anger. They stared at the ground, the men standing, the women sitting.

The President asked again, and the old woman elaborated her story, weaving in the bright details as though she were making the fringe of a tunic. Her hands fumbled with stones on the ground.

Her husband is dead, she lives on little. When the boy came to ask for her daughter, she didn't want to, but she let them marry. Yes, the boy brought the wedding gifts. He brought liquor, bananas. He brought bread, meat, cigarettes which she gave away to her brother. Yes, the girl was happy to marry him, and they went away to live in the house of the boy's father. Within a few months the boy had a little piece of land and built a house of his own. The girl had a baby. Then for no reason the husband went home to his father's house, leaving the girl alone. She had no corn to make tortillas, she had no beans to eat, no vegetables, no greens. She came home to her mother's house. Now the boy was petitioning for another girl who lived nearby. He would not give his wife the things to eat, or for the baby. And the old woman herself is poor, she has only enough food for herself.

The President lit another cigarette, crossed his legs and spat on the ground. Other officials had come and crowded onto the cement bench. Some of the scribes, the young officials, arrived and leaned over the back of the bench, talking to each other. Like the buzz of flies.

"And why did the husband go home?" the President asked the old woman.

She shook her head, and dropped her shawl. She did not know. The boy just did it.

The husband began to laugh to himself, and then his own father laughed. When the old woman looked up at them, her eyes betrayed her bitterness.

Hearing laughter, the baby laughed, and its mother pulled her shawl over its face. She hoped it would go to sleep.

"President," the husband said, "that old woman knows why I went home. Everyone knows. I told them all. The girl does not know how to sleep with me. It's true, she doesn't."

The laughter began with the scribes. They punched one another and hooted. The officials chuckled, bobbing in their seats. The President himself enjoyed the joke and he looked at the husband to be sure it was a joke. But the boy's face was blank, his eyes were wide with his own excitement. His smile was deceptive, so the President found no clue to the truth.

"Let her watch sheep to learn," called one of the scribes to another.

"Let her come watch you and your wife," said the other, and the laughter came in new waves.

"All right." The President cleared his throat, and his leg bounced with impatience. The joke was not as good as that. "Then where does the baby come from? Isn't it yours?"

He pointed at the child, now almost asleep, just a bulge in his mother's shawl. The girl kept her eyes cast down, as though she were carefully examining the flies eating the President's spittle.

The father of the husband came forward. He pulled out a pack of cigarettes and offered one to the President. The President accepted, putting the cigarette in his own pack. "President," said the man, "it is not the boy's child. It was some stranger who came and stayed at her house. A man she knew, my son did not know him."

"How old is your son?"

"I don't know. Maybe sixteen, maybe seventeen."

"Maybe," said the President deliberately, "it is your son who does not know how to sleep with a woman." He himself began the laughter now, and he let it run up and down the bench.

The old woman was temporarily satisfied. She laughed and said "Huh!" Even the girl smiled, though she hid it behind her shawl.

"Here, take the boy to San Martín. Take him to the White Bridge," one of the scribes called out. The other scribes laughed again. The White Bridge in town was the place for prostitutes. Some of them, the old ones, would sleep with Indians.

"Let him spend·the night in your house," said another scribe.

The boy in question came to the President and bowed. The President released him, and the boy said he *did* know how to sleep with women. But there was the stranger. His wife said the man was her brother, but the husband did not believe it.

"Then the child is not yours?" the President asked.

"Yes, it is my child."

The officials stirred and whispered to one another, their interest in the case renewed.

"My father doesn't know. It is my child. Not that my wife doesn't know how to sleep with a man, but she doesn't know how to make tortillas, she doesn't know how to make my food, how to make my clothes. I had to go home or I would have starved."

The old woman crept closer to the President. She said

that none of the accusations was true. The daughter knew how to cook, and to spin. The daughter had made that very tunic for the boy.

"Let's see," the President said, beckoning the boy to him. The tunic was a thick one, good wool, with wide-spaced pink and green stripes and good long fringe at the bottom. He asked the daughter if she made this. He spoke kindly since tears were rolling down the girl's dirty cheeks. Muffling her voice with the shawl, the girl said she made the tunic.

"My mother made it. That girl does not even know how to weave!" said the boy, pulling away from the President. The President asked, and the boy's mother also claimed that she made the tunic.

They had reached an impasse, and the President was bored. Each side would now repeat its story over and over. Finally the President would make a decision which would satisfy no one, least of all himself, because he did not trust his own judgment. Whenever a case was brought to him he hoped there would be a single shaded path for him, one answer to each of his questions, and a single judgment so clear the others would see it coming before he even said the words.

The President only half listened. The boy's mother was telling how she took the wool from her own sheep to make him the tunic, because he came home from his married life almost in rags. And thin, for he had barely eaten.

The wife was crying, or perhaps it was the baby who cried. Yes, it was the baby, for the girl slipped her hand into the slit under the arm of her blouse and pushed the nipple into the baby's face. The baby refused and the girl squeezed a little until her nipple was softened and wet. Finally the crying stopped.

The other officials were quiet, staring at their feet, swatting flies, dozing off to sleep. Some of the scribes drifted away uninterested. Or they began to play, pushing into each other, joking.

All of the people from the hamlet talked at once. The President told them several times to shut up. The others did eventually, but the boy's mother continued her high singsong complaint.

"Shut up!" said the President vehemently. The old woman did. "Now then," he continued, "the boy is unsatisfied with his wife. She does not know how to cook his food, weave his clothes. So he goes home, and now is petitioning for a new wife. Well. He can do that."

The officials were awake and attentive. The President wondered why they cared. They had heard the same case, the same judgment many times.

The boy in question smiled at his father. The old woman had stopped fumbling with stones. She listened carefully.

The girl's shawl had fallen from her head. The baby lay exposed to the sun and untended. Soon, thought the President, it will begin squalling again. The girl was drawing breath heavily. Well, the President thought, looking at the two women, they probably tell the truth. They were dirty. No one had denied the old woman's husband was dead. The baby's hair was long and matted. Crusted with a scabby kind of dirt on his forehead, from sitting too close to the fire unwatched.

"But—but—" said the President loudly, waving his finger in the air, bobbing his foot, addressing the line of officials seated on either side of him, "but the girl has nothing to eat. Her mother cannot give her corn, or even beans. Someone must pay or she will starve."

Several officials nodded wisely in agreement.

"So the husband must provide for her. How much?" the President asked, turning to the officials beside him.

He did not know himself. He took out a notebook and a ballpoint pen, found a clean page, and played with figures for a moment. The figures were meaningless, but they gave him time enough to think. "A hundred and fifty pesos."

The old woman had hidden her despair, but now she could not hide her elation. She crawled to him and bowed her head for his touch. He released her. The girl did not seem affected, and she continued to breathe heavily. The son's smile was gone.

"But President, I'm a young man. I don't have that money. I don't have land, I don't grow much corn."

"Maybe you should not marry so soon again then," said the President. He had expected the storm from the boy's side, and waited for it to descend on him. When they began shouting he stared at his notebook and continued writing numbers. Sometimes his writing silenced people from the hamlets, and made them afraid.

When the boy and his father ran out of things to say, the President took their names and the name of the old woman and her daughter. He wrote down the name of their hamlet, and the amount. Then he explained to the old woman that she could come to him with a complaint if the boy did not pay her in two weeks. She thanked him, and bowed again. She bowed to the other officials, they touched her head, the girl's head, then the two left the courtyard. The boy's family, of course, was unsatisfied. But the President knew this would happen, and he no longer even attempted to hear the things they were saying. He stood and stretched and grunted and then wandered away onto the porch of the Cabildo. It was ten o'clock but already he was stiff and tired.

Since no one was listening to them any more, the boy and his family began to gather their bags and children, and left.

The Maestro from the school met the President, and said good morning in Tzotzil.

"What's going on at the school this morning?" the President asked.

"I don't understand," the Maestro said, falling back into Spanish.

The President didn't offer to translate.

"What language do the Indians speak there where you come from?"

"In Oaxaca?"

"Yes."

"I don't know the names," the Maestro said, scratching his head.

"Is the talk as hard as our Tzotzil?"

"I don't know. I never tried to learn."

The President nodded, understanding. "Do you know about the Lacandones?" he asked suddenly.

The Maestro did not.

"They live south of here. Many days away, in hot country. In the jungles, not in the mountains like we do." The President pointed to the south. "They don't wear clothes because it's so hot."

"Oh, yes." The Maestro nodded. "I have heard of them."

"The men have hair down to here, to the belt. Like women," the President explained. "And they kill with arrows. They put them in sugar-cane pipes, and blow them at you like this." The President demonstrated and then laughed.

"And—" But he had reached the end of his memory.

The Maestro continued nodding, agreeing it was all true.

The President enjoyed talking this way with the Maestro. The flavor of it reminded him of his own time as schoolmaster. Or of an even earlier time when he himself went to the Indian Institute in San Martín to learn the business of teaching. When he spent days with photographs and colored maps. He would trace a journey through the states of Mexico, matching the names of towns with pictures in the book. Then he would find every detail in every picture, and at the end of a day would go to his meal and bed worn out, as though he had actually returned from a trip. Never did he feel exhilarated with his new knowledge; the journeys were painful and exhausting. Yet he went to the library day after day.

One time the men at the Institute took him to Mexico City for five weeks. He wore their clothes and spoke Spanish until his mouth was tired from the strange words. He rode in a soft-cushioned seat on the bus, and could not sleep. When he got to Mexico City he would not give in and show the Institute men how excited he was, because he did not really feel any excitement. He took the city in small pictures, and examined them like the photographs in the library. He comprehended it in slow draughts, never in great gulps. And coming home to Chiapas he was more exhausted than ever. When he had made the long return trip south from Mexico City and was safely back in the Institute station in San Martín, he did not even think of the City for several weeks.

Since then, since he had been Maestro at Cruztik and President, he no longer gave much time to the memory of Mexico City. Sometimes the hum of the traffic would flood his dreams at night, or the taste of bread he bought in San Martín would remind him of things he had eaten in Mexico City. But he did not miss it.

The Maestro had been in Mexico City, he had been on the bus to San Martín. He had been born in Oaxaca. And this created a bond between them. The President did not talk of Mexico City, but when the Maestro did, the President understood. It was like an open secret. They would explain to the others, but there was never a guarantee the others would understand. It was a range of knowledge they held in common, and which they could not exchange or sell to others.

The President had heard the Maestro explaining to Mario, his friend, about Mexico City, and knew the Maestro's disappointment. He had tried the same thing with his son Eliseo. Eliseo had all the education and knowledge the President could give him, but it was not enough. The President was resolved that his son should see the City. It would be a bond between them.

The Maestro waited for the President to go on, but the President was silent.

He recalled the pictures still, but the details had faded. He had more to say, but seemed to have lost the words. Then a coughing spell overtook him, and he walked away from the Maestro, trying to shake it off.

Wearing a clean cotton coat and looking debonair, the Doctor came striding across the plaza from the infirmary, followed by Mario.

The Doctor went inside the Cabildo to use the old battery-powered wall telephone which was the only quick connection between Chomtik and the outside world. To begin the long process of trying to rouse San Martín, he ground the handle furiously to make the bell chirrup, and

shouted "Martín!—Martín!" into the mouthpiece. With
real luck he might get the thin, strained voice from the
Indian Institute in five minutes, and in another ten he
might get to talk with the person he was calling.

Mario saw the Doctor would be busy, and thought of
running his errand. But instead he talked to the Maestro.

"How are you?" the Maestro said slowly in Tzotzil.

"Well enough," answered Mario in Spanish.

"Is your father better?"

"No, not much."

"I was thinking of coming home with you in the evening, but if your father is still sick—"

"No, come on," said Mario, smiling.

One of the officials, who had arrived late for the morning's business, had stopped to listen to the two men talk.
When they paused, he said good morning to Mario in
Tzotzil, and since the official was old, Mario bowed to him
and the official touched him lightly on the head, releasing
him.

He was a Second Alcalde, a man of minor importance.
Small and wiry, he had thick-tufted eyebrows and a bris-
tling mustache of a few long hairs. He cocked his head
and asked Mario what the Maestro had said, since he himself did not speak Spanish except when he had to.

"He's asking permission to come to my house. He's trying to learn how to talk the way we do."

"Why?"

"I don't know. So he can talk to the children at the
school."

The official obviously didn't believe the story. "You had
better watch for your wife. That's what the *hkashlan*
wants."

"No," said Mario, "he has his own woman there in the
school."

"Oh." The Second Alcalde nodded, admitting his error. "Does he know how to eat the food at your house?" Mario nodded. "He does? Well. And to drink *posh*, does he know that?" Mario nodded again. "He does? Well. And where does he sleep?"

"On the floor," Mario said.

"On the floor! Why not on the bed, not as many fleas there."

"Well," said Mario, "he won't take the bed away from me."

"No, just the woman in the bed." The Second Alcalde laughed, wrinkling his nose like a rabbit. "Watch out for *hkashlan*," he warned. Then he smiled at the Maestro again, and went away.

The Maestro had heard this word *hkashlan*, and asked Mario what it meant.

"*Hkashlan?* It means outsider, anyone who isn't an Indian," Mario explained in Spanish. "Anyone who screws the poor Indians," he added a minute later.

The Maestro laughed, glad that Mario was now secure enough with him to say these things.

"A Ladino."

The Maestro nodded.

At the other end of the Cabildo porch was the jail. Two of the Maestro's schoolboys crept around the corner, laughing over some great secret. One pulled the other toward the heavy latticed door. They leaned against the bars a moment, staring into the dark, and then ran away.

"Who's in the jail?" the Maestro asked Mario.

Mario smiled his bright smile and said, "Who knows?"

"I'll go see," said the Maestro, starting off toward the other end of the porch.

"Look!" Mario called after him. "Here comes Jacinto's truck!" And Mario walked quickly out into the plaza to watch the beautiful stubby red truck with the yellow tarpaulin as it rounded the hill at one end of the valley and began the long easy glide down to the plaza. Actually the truck belonged to the Indian Institute, but since Jacinto drove it the Indians called it his.

Jacinto always brought his truck into the village slowly, almost grandly. Though the road was good, Jacinto took his time, riding the clutch in low gear.

The Maestro gave up his trip to the jail and went out into the sun to see who the magnificent new truck would deposit in front of Jacinto's store.

Jacinto had reached the bottom of the hill and now came up over a little rise into the plaza. He always put on speed to do this, and then had to slam on the brakes in front of his store. It was a flourish, a bit of bravura like a flashy signature.

The officials were standing to look out over the plaza from behind their cement bench, soldiers at a rampart. Even the President was interested. He saw Jacinto leap out of the cab and greet Eliseo, who always waited in front of the store. Then Jacinto strutted around to the red nose of his truck, threw open the hood and inspected his engine.

He was always cocky, thought the President, in his Mexican clothes with tennis shoes and a baseball cap, and always wearing the smile of a proud dishonest child on his round face.

At the back end of the truck Jacinto's helper, Antun, jumped down and pulled out a ladder. Antun wore Mexican clothes also, but was not so proud. He didn't strut when he walked. An Indian came down the ladder first, carrying a white satchel. Then came three Mexican boys, who lit cigarettes as soon as they reached the ground, and who seemed from a distance to be reluctant to pay Antun the peso apiece they owed him for the ride. When they had finally handed over the money, they started walking toward the Cabildo, heads bent together in secret conversation.

The last passenger in the back of the truck was a young-looking Indian woman. Antun helped her down and then scrambled into the truck to bring out her belongings. She had a lot of them—a wooden box, two or three burlap bags, and finally a pure white lamb with its feet tied together. Antun carried each of these possessions to the door of the store beside Jacinto's.

Jacinto climbed down from the front end of the truck and went to open the cab door for his other rider. The man who got out was an Indian, but tall for an Indian. He wore Indian clothes, but the clothes, the hat, even the leather bag were all clean, new. He spoke briefly to Jacinto and to Antun, who did not try to collect his peso from the man. Then, going to the ramshackle store where the woman waited, the man unlocked the door and disappeared inside. The woman lugged the bundles inside and closed the door after her.

The officials buzzed, heads bent so that hats almost touched. The scribes, in their different, more confident way, made jokes. The Maestro was not quite sure why.

"Who's that?" he asked Mario.

"Juan López Oso has come back," Mario said, and then laughed. "With his woman."

"What's funny about that?"

"Well, she's not the same woman Oso had before he went away."

The Maestro laughed too, and then Mario excused himself, and loped off across the plaza toward the church. The

Maestro could hear a rising hubbub of young voices coming from his school and went to contend with disorder.

One of the scribes who spoke Spanish met the three
Mexican boys when they came onto the porch.

"Where's the man in charge?" demanded one of the
boys.

"The President is there," the scribe said, nodding toward the bench in the courtyard. All the officials and the
President were watching.

"Not the fucking Indian, where's the Secretary?"

The President pretended he had not heard this, and the
scribe, still smiling, went to bring Don Concepción, who
led the boys into the cool office. There they lit new cigarettes and gave one to the Secretary, and then they explained how the blackhearted Indians had stolen a mule
they brought to sell a week ago during the fiesta of San
Sebastián.

When Don Concepción gave no promises to see that
justice was done them, that their mule would be returned,
they offered him twenty pesos in crumpled bills if he
would retrieve their stolen property. Don Concepción
eyed their money over his glasses, then looked at their
flushed faces one by one to see how much they had had to
drink in order to steel themselves before they came out
from San Martín. They were a little drunk.

"Look here," said the oldest of the boys as he repocketed
the bills, "I came all the way up from Flores to get either
my money or the animal. My uncle is in the government
there. My father is a well-known man. I'm not here to
waste my time."

Don Concepción nodded, admitting the truth that no
one ever wanted to waste time. He thought to himself that
the son of an important legislator in the state capital

doesn't waste his time coming up in the mountains to cheat a bunch of Indians out of a single mule. But Don Concepción pretended to believe the lie and took the Mexican boys out in the sun to talk to the President.

Don Concepción explained the situation to the President, and then withdrew to his own house to attend to his screaming grandson. The boys filled in the details for the President in hurried, nervous sentences, while the officials watched these strangers, unable to comprehend what they wanted.

The President beckoned one of the scribes and sent him off to fetch someone.

While they waited the Mexican boys sat on the cement bench, and watched the strange savages around them. The Mexicans had taken the President's seat, and he paced across the courtyard, thinking to himself, and muttering under his breath.

When the scribe returned, trotting, he was followed by an old woman with gray hair whose tattered skirt flapped behind her as she ran toward the Cabildo, already angry and shouting.

The President met her in the courtyard and, still standing, presented the Mexican boys' case to her. She was a mulekeeper and the boys claimed they had seen their mule grazing with her small herd as they rode into the village on the truck.

But how did they come to lose their precious mule? the President asked.

Well, they explained, some Indians had gotten them drunk in the fiesta, and when they got back to San Martín they discovered they had lost their mule. It must have been the old woman who stole it.

She denied all this, when the President translated for

her. She lived here in the Center, she said. She was a widow and her whole life depended on her dozen mules.

She was angry and ready to argue. As she talked the Mexican boys stared at her with smirks on their faces. No longer afraid, they were impatient with these people. They told the President what the mule was like—it had a scar across its back, its tail was cut fancy to look like three tassels hanging below one another.

As they explained in Spanish, the old woman went on talking in Tzotzil. When she saw the President was not listening to her, she appealed to the mute officials.

On the other side of the plaza, Jacinto had climbed back into his red truck and had given a merry toot on the horn to announce his departure for San Martín. He started the motor and moved out to make a turn in the plaza.

One of the town boys saw him and ran to stop the truck, to persuade Jacinto to wait for them. The boy bribed Jacinto with cigarettes, and Jacinto cut his motor. The other two Mexicans went out into the valley with the old woman to retrieve the disputed mule, and many of the officials, having nothing to do, went with them.

When they returned with a handsome gray animal, the President inspected it closely. Bobbed, carefully cut tail, and the scar running from the neck down the left side. As the woman continued pleading, telling where she had bought the mule, how she walked it up from Esperanza herself, how she had cared for it, the President admitted in Spanish that the mule belonged to the Mexicans. The boys were jubilant and shouted the decision to their friend waiting beside Jacinto's truck.

"But," the President added, "the woman here has cared for your mule for two weeks, and you must pay her for that."

"How much?" Having won, the boys were anxious to leave.

"Forty pesos."

Both boys laughed, quick thin laughs which they barely forced out between their lips. "Thirty," said one, pulling the wadded bills from his pocket.

The President took these, carefully unfolding and smoothing each one before putting it away under his tunic. The old woman did not seem to understand what was going on, but she stopped talking when she saw the money disappear into the President's pocket.

The Mexicans escaped with their prize, leading the mule quickly out to Jacinto's waiting truck. Antun put down the ladder, but it proved almost too steep for the mule. Antun and the three Mexicans pushed the mule's rump again and again, as it resisted. Jacinto had started the motor again, and each time he roared the engine, the mule tried to back down. When it finally gave in, it went so quickly that two of the boys fell headlong onto the ground. The officials laughed, and even the President smiled. The old woman was talking fast now, but she was silenced when the President gave her the money.

Jacinto's truck pulled out with the thin faces of the three Chickens from town leering out the back.

The President calculated the woman's loss: the mule might be worth six hundred pesos; she had received thirty. He felt sorry for her, sorry that he couldn't take the chance of defying the Mexicans. But the woman had accepted the money he gave her so quickly. Maybe the lie was hers, not the Mexicans'. The President couldn't tell.

4   Mario

THE SUN WAS HIGH AND
hot, and black clouds were creeping over the mountain
from the east. At the top of the church's high façade were
three arched openings, containing three bells. Now an Indian appeared on the roof and came to strike the bell in
the center with a hammer. It was already noon and when
the sound of the bell reached them, the officials took off
their hats.

Like a rabbit frightened by the clang, Mario darted out
of the low door of the church, and came back to the Cabildo running. The Doctor, through with his phone call,
was waiting.

"Where were you? I've been waiting."

"I was at the church," Mario said, knowing the Doctor
had seen him come out and that he could not lie.

"Praying?" asked the Doctor.

They had a good laugh over that one. Early in their
friendship the Doctor had confided to his assistant that he
did not believe in God. Instead of being upset, Mario had
promptly admitted that he did not believe either.

"I went to tell the sacristan it was time to ring the bell,"
Mario explained. "He has no watch."

The Doctor looked down at Mario's wrist, at the watch
he had given his assistant, the watch that was better than
even the President's.

"Well, come on then. Let's get our instruments and go
cut up the meat." The Doctor started out for the infirmary,
taking long strides which Mario couldn't match.

Mario wanted to share his satisfaction with someone immediately. He looked around, but the Maestro was not there, so Mario was forced to follow the man he could not tell.

He had gone to the church to talk to the curer the Doctor had asked about earlier. He had waited in the cool gigantic darkness of the church for what seemed like hours, while the little group stood before the altar rail and the curer mumbled prayers to the large statue of the Patrón San Juan. Mario crept closer, down the wide aisle between the lines of the other, lesser saints, who stared down at him with their calm white-painted faces.

The old curer left candles burning before the altar, and moved his little group so it was facing San Jermino, the patron of souls. The crying women and the sick man sat while the curer addressed the saint. Mario waited and watched impatiently. At last the curer began to sweep away the pine needles on the stone floor, and planted a row of white tapers. The glow of the candles sealed off the group from Mario, and as he stared into the flames, the whole church seemed darker, as though night had come. The curer laid out flowers—white crumpled roses and purple air plant—and then summoned the sick man's son to him. The boy poured little glasses of clear liquor, while the curer lined them up before the candles. One glass was poured out on the floor for the saint, and then the curer drank a glass. Another was offered to the sick man, who tasted it and gagged, and handed the glass back. Then the curer looked around, and saw Mario standing near him. He beckoned and Mario took the *posh*, thanked the curer and the sick man, and drank. He was unprepared for the raw sting of it, since for a long time he had drunk only the Ladinos' stuff, which was always smooth. This was bitter, but a vague sweetness from it hung in his mouth afterwards.

The curer seemed to forget anyone was with him as the others drank—the boy who poured and then the curer's wife and the sick man's woman and younger children.

Mario was afraid to interrupt, but now felt strongly the need to speak and get back before the Doctor missed him.

"Older brother?" he whispered.

The curer was drunk, and did not hear him. Mario got up and then squatted so close to the curer that their shoulders touched.

"Older brother." Now when he spoke the curer bent his head to listen. "My father is sick. Will you do me the favor, please?"

"What favor?"

"Will you come listen to what his blood says? Will you make him well?"

The curer nodded several times. "I can come the day after tomorrow, in the afternoon."

Another glass of liquor was passed to the curer. He drank it in a single gulp and shivered, and his whole body seemed to respond to the *posh*. He was an older man, gray hair like fringe stuck out from beneath the white bandanna he wore wrapped around his head. He was a famous curer, and Mario had approached him in fear and desperation.

Mario took a small bottle of red vermouth out of the leather bag which he carried under his medical smock. He begged the curer to take the bottle, and the curer accepted the gift, which meant he would come to see Mario's father. The curer took the empty glass in his other hand, uncorked the bottle with his teeth, and poured a drink of the vermouth for Mario. Mario insisted that the curer drink first, which he did. Then Mario poured himself a glass, and thanked the curer again. When he drank he could barely taste the vermouth, it was so sweet and weak, and the taste of the *posh* stayed in his mouth.

Following the Doctor across the plaza, Mario hoped the autopsy would not take long. He hoped the Doctor would find whatever it was he looked for in the guts quickly. Then the Doctor would go away to town to see his mistress, and Mario could close the infirmary and get home to Lumtik to tell his father the curer would come soon.

5 The Boy

HAVING SOLVED THE PROBLEM of the mules, the President decided he would go home at once for his meal and a short sleep. But instead curiosity drew him to the black doorway of the jail. Several of the officials followed the President and stood on the edge of the stone porch while the President went to the door and stared into the dark. At first he could barely make out the form of the dead man in the straw. If he had not known the truth it would have seemed only that the man was sleeping, curled up with his legs against his chest to keep out the cold. The stench was there, but it might be just the smell of straw and the jail.

The boy was huddled against the back wall, squatting with his head almost between his knees. When the President called him, he looked up, then he came to the door, and pressed his face into one of the openings. The officials came a little closer to watch.

Flush against the wooden bars, the boy's face was distorted. His eyes were clouded and two lines of yellow dirt streaked down his cheeks.

"Maestro?" the boy said under his breath.

"Yes?"

"Maestro, what are they going to do with me?" Tears had formed again in the boy's eyes.

The President thought while reaching for a cigarette. He recognized the boy, he could remember what the father looked like alive, a smiling, indolent, almost childish man with a big house several hills away from the school in Cruztik. This boy himself never learned quickly, but he played basketball, and several times had asked the President what Mexico City was like. Not with the longing for the strange which only a very few of the boys had, but with a frightened and anxious curiosity.

It seemed to the President that little had changed. The boy's question about his fate was almost like his questions about Mexico City three years ago. The President could form the answers in his mind, but at the same time an intense weariness would crowd his head. There was no use explaining things the boy would never really understand.

"You will be put in Santo Domingo—in the jail." The President found his cigarette and lit it.

The boy watched closely, and a sigh like the rustle of straw escaped from him.

"But they will kill me, isn't that true?"

"Who will?"

"The *hkashlan* in town."

"No. There is no death for crimes in Mexico."

"But I did kill my father."

The boy's mouth was distended, pulled down because

he was pressing so tight against the wooden bars, and his voice was a whisper.

"Why did you do that?"

"I was drunk, Maestro."

The President shook his head and murmured the word *lastimó,* pity, under his breath.

The officials standing behind the President shook their heads in sadness and understanding.

"My father sent me away to work on fincas in hot country, Maestro, he is very poor and he sent me away because he's old. I went in September, after the fiesta of San Mateo, and I stayed there to work in the coffee plantations four months. I wanted to come home, but I stayed in hot country. Then on Sunday I came home. My father was happy, and my mother. I was tired and sick and I drank with my father, he bought the liquor because he was glad. When we finished one liter he sent my younger brother to buy more. I didn't want to drink so much, but I had to because of my father. He was drunk and then I was drunk. Even my mother. Then I told my father I wanted to marry. I have watched the girl, she lives near my father's house in Cruztik. My father had all the money I brought from finca, and I asked him to give me money to buy the gifts for the girl's father. I had worked hard for my father. Look!"

The boy stuck a hand out through the cagework of the door. The hand was thickly calloused, and on the fingers there was blood.

The President had thrown away his cigarette and had his own hands folded beneath his tunic. They felt thin and almost useless. He knew he could not expect his old hands to be as strong as the boy's, but still he regretted his own weakness. Because he was a teacher and then President, he had not farmed corn, worked with a hoe, for many years. He could barely remember the feel of his hands tight around the handle, or the shock that runs through a man's arms when the hoe sinks into the ground. Maybe, the President thought, his sickness—the heaviness in his chest, the unpleasant sensation of exhaustion which followed him through each day—all of it might go away if he were free to work his own land and to live his own life again. More than ever he wanted to shed himself of the Presidency.

"Maestro," the boy continued, "for all the work I could have all the money I need to marry. But I gave what I saved to my father instead, and he refused to pay for the girl. He said no, when I asked him, said my work was still for him, that I could not marry. We were drunk, Maestro. I took a rope and hit him then. I was drunk. My long machete was lying by the door. I tried to hit my father with that, Maestro!"

The boy had been crying as he spoke, and the President listened staring at the ground. He could see what had happened, he felt he understood what had seemed impossible the night before—how a boy could kill his father.

He could almost hear what he would say when he explained all this to Don Roberto, the lawyer in San Martín who would take the case to court. He could hear himself forming the words in Spanish, and could see Don Roberto's friendly, even stare. The President admired this Mexican, for he never betrayed surprise at what Indians had done, he never seemed to feel uneasy about what to do as the President did.

But for all his interest, and in this case even for his pity, Don Roberto would probably be thinking, Crazy Indians, drunk and killing all the time.

The President wished that in his own retelling of the story he could have the power to let Don Roberto see it as he had just seen it. But that was too much like explaining Mexico City to the school children or to Eliseo.

"Maestro!"

"What?"

"I was drunk."

"I understand," he said.

The boy was asking for something, something the President could feel but could not name. But he knew he could not give it to the boy.

"Forgive me, Maestro, I was drunk."

This made the President angry and he decided to leave the boy. "I can't do that," he muttered. "I can't do that," he repeated louder. "Do you think I'm Our Father?"

A jeep had turned off the main road at the top of the valley, and now was buzzing down the hill and into the village. It was one of the Indian Institute's cars, and calmly, as though he had rehearsed this scene, the Maestro sauntered out of his school to meet the visitors. At the same time the Doctor, also nonchalant, came out on the porch of the infirmary, still in his pure white laboratory coat.

The driver of the jeep got out and opened the door for a squat Mexican in a brown suit, who stretched when he got out of the car. He was followed by his plump wife and plumper daughter.

The President hoped it wouldn't be necessary for him to greet the city people, and turned back to the boy to shield himself. He always felt like a puppet or an especially fine horse the Institute owned when these visitors came.

"Do you have a trade, something you know how to make?" he asked the boy.

"My father makes guitars. I know how to make them."

The President thought a moment and shook his head. "No. You will have to learn in Santo Domingo. They let you sell what you make in the daytime, and you keep the money. But the people in San Martín don't want our guitars. Can you make net bags?"

"No."

The President shook his head again, thinking of the line of Indian criminals who sat every day along the pastel blue wall of the Santo Domingo courtyard, sewing bags. The boy would be there for a long time. Without a trade he wouldn't die. But with a trade he could eat better.

The President turned his attention to the city visitors the Institute had sent. He was relieved when the Doctor greeted them only briefly and left them to come to the jail.

"Is that the guy?" asked the Doctor when he came onto the porch.

"Yes."

"Huh! Doesn't look old enough to be a killer. Why did he do it, hate his father?"

"No," said the President, "they were drunk and they fought, that's all."

"Oh, I see."

Living in the village, the Doctor had the opportunity to understand this better than Don Roberto in San Martín could. But, the President thought bitterly, the difference was that the Doctor did not care to understand.

"I'm going to take the body out now and start working on it," the Doctor said.

With the President he went around to the doorway of the Cabildo. Inside the office Don Concepción and the Maestro were talking to the three visitors. The President picked a few scribes to go along to the autopsy, and sent them to the storeroom to get a bucket, some shovels and a hacksaw. The President told the policemen who were there that they had to go along to dig the grave.

Then the man named Salvador arrived at the Cabildo with Juan López Oso. The President told Salvador he would have to go along too, since he brought in the body.

"You've come back." The President smiled slightly when he turned to Juan López Oso.

"Yes." Oso also smiled, showing his three expensive gold teeth. He was a tall, strong man, almost forty. His nose was long, his eyes big and dark. He always moved and spoke with urgency, there was a kind of overwhelming strength about him. When he drank he was frightening, for then his violence was freed.

"Where did you go?"

"To Flores with my new woman."

The President had known Oso a long time. He had been a friend of Oso's father, but he hadn't been sure he could ask about the new woman.

"Where's your wife?"

"The old one?" Oso asked. "She's still at my house in Lumtik."

Oso was a wealthy man there, probably the richest man in the hamlet aside from the President. But since Oso had become a permanent official, the liaison with the Institute's schools, he had opened a store in the village and lived in the back of it much of the time.

"I have to have someone with me here, to make my meals and to screw." Oso's eyes shone. "The old woman has the children, and I needed a woman here, alone."

The President said nothing, but coughed and spat on the ground. Oso made him feel weak.

"Don't worry, President. I have the money for both of

them." Oso laughed. "They won't go hungry. I have that strength."

He could sense the President's disapproval and it made him mad. But he was just back, he had expected the disapproval, and was determined for once not to show his anger.

"Will you come to my house to eat?" asked the President, looking up at the sun. It was late and he was hungry.

"No, President, thanks. I want to watch the Doctor cut up the dead man."

The Maestro came out of the office, followed by his three plump guests.

"Ho, Juan!" the Maestro called. He went to Oso, took the Indian's hand, and reached up to embrace him.

"They told me it was you who had come."

"Yes, I've come."

"How was Flores?"

"Good."

"Are you going to live there?"

"No, I just took my new woman, we went to look around."

"Here," the Maestro went on hurriedly, remembering he had not made the proper introductions. "Señor Medina, this is Juan López Oso, the Chomtik Chief of Schools."

Señor Medina bowed slightly and took the hand which Oso offered him. "Delighted," said the Mexican. "My wife and daughter." The woman smiled and the girl blushed.

"And did you meet the President?" asked the Maestro, remembering himself again.

Señor Medina was again delighted and shook hands.

"Señor Medina is the Institute's Director of Education for the State of Hidalgo."

The President smiled.

"And the President was formerly a schoolteacher for the Institute," the Maestro went on to explain. Again Señor Medina was delighted.

"And how long have you been President?" he asked.

"Two years."

"I see," said Señor Medina, stroking his round chin. "The officials don't change every year here in Chomtik."

The Maestro explained. "Well, most of them do. The rest of the men you saw this morning. But the Institute thought that for the sake of continuity one man should continue in the job of President for several years. And the same with the Chief of Schools. But effectually we don't have any control over the other civil positions. The Indians fill them by themselves, along traditional lines which are of pre-Conquest origin."

Señor Medina nodded sagely. "Then the Institute provides the President these days?" he said.

"Oh, no," the Maestro said quickly. "The Indian government is completely autonomous here, completely. Neither the Secretary nor I, nor the people at the Institute in San Martín—none of us—interfere in the government here."

"Well, then," Señor Medina said, turning to the President, "it must be a great honor and satisfaction to be chosen by your people for this job."

"Yes," the President agreed. "It is."

"And who will succeed you?"

The President didn't understand the city man's Spanish, and looked to the Maestro.

"Well, actually we don't know yet," said the Maestro. "That will be decided in the summer, since this President has decided not to take the office a fourth year. Maybe"—

the Maestro smiled—"maybe Juan here would like to be President." The Maestro put a friendly arm on Oso's shoulder.

"I see. Very interesting," Señor Medina said, to signal he had had enough of this conversation.

They walked together out into the plaza. The clouds from the east had almost caught up with the sun. But it didn't look to the President as though they would bring rain. At least not immediately.

The scribes and the policemen were waiting with their shovels and the bucket. The jail door had been swung open and the body was being strapped again to the bent back of the boy. As he tottered forward, out into the plaza, the three Mexican visitors stopped dead and the women's faces were masks of shock.

Squat Señor Medina let out a grunt. His daughter put her hands to her face and hid in the warm corner of her mother's shoulder. The Doctor, who had seen all this, ran to make amends.

"I'm terribly sorry, sir, I didn't mean you to be subjected to this."

"No, no, it's all right," said Señor Medina nervously. "Is the poor man diseased?"

"He's dead."

"My God!" The Indian Institute's Director of Education for the State of Hidalgo pulled a handkerchief from his breast pocket, and put it to his face. His wife crossed herself with her free hand.

"We're going to bury him now."

"Did he just die?" asked the wife.

"No, he was murdered by his son there."

"That boy carrying him? Mother of God!" Señor Medina wiped his brow and then his jowls. "And you have to go?"

"I have to perform the autopsy, according to law," the Doctor said courageously.

"You poor man," sighed the daughter.

Beside Señor Medina, the Maestro waited impatiently.

The Doctor was pleased. He had stolen whatever little glory the Maestro had gained by showing off the school and his knowledge of Indian life. The Maestro might lead visitors around all he wanted, pointing out the interesting little mushroom patches of useless learning he had cultivated on top of the little Indian minds. But now the Doctor felt he had plucked out the bleeding misery of the savage heart and held it up, still pulsing with life-in-death for the visitors to see. They would not forget this, the *coup de grâce* of their morning in Chomtik.

The more the Doctor watched the growing discomfort of the Maestro, the more he wanted to take Señor Medina aside and tell him that the Maestro and the female teacher at the school were living in sin. But the Doctor desisted, deciding that such gossip was beneath him. He begged the visitors' pardon for upsetting them and strode off at the end of the burial procession.

The killer had stopped before the President, like a mule before its master. The boy was bent over and did not look up from under his burden. His tears had begun again, but he no longer sobbed.

No one knew why he waited, and several of the scribes told him to move on.

Then the President took out his pack of Alas and held it before the boy. The boy's arms were up over his shoulders supporting the chair. Seeing this, the President took out a

cigarette, put it in the boy's mouth, and lit it with the butt
of his own. The boy breathed in, and started moving.

Several people saw what the President did, and it gave
them a moment's wonder. The President never shared his
own cigarettes as everyone else did.

6   Juan López Oso

THE SCRIBES LED THE
way, followed by the policemen with the shovels and the
bucket, and Juan López Oso with the man named Salvador, and last the Doctor with Mario.

As they were tramping up the road to the abandoned
church of San Sebastián and the cemetery, the scribes
talked of other things—of their wives, of the three Mexican
boys who reclaimed the mule, of what it would be like to
make love to the Mexican visitor's chubby wife. The man
Salvador kept silent, expecting his new brother-in-law Oso
would soon explain what was about to happen. But Oso
had nothing to say.

The Doctor concentrated on the noble impression he
had made on the Mexican visitors, and then thought of the
afternoon he would spend with his mistress in San Martín,
once he had finished this business.

Only Mario, and perhaps the boy, thought of what was
coming. As he jogged along beside his boss, Mario kept
his eyes on the bloody head of the murdered man, already
seeing the line he would draw with his knife when he
turned back the scalp.

The abandoned church of San Sebastián was four great
walls with no roof. The grass grew high, since sheep did

not dare enter to graze, and the sound of crickets echoed off the old stone. Nothing but the size remained to say for sure it had ever been a church. Within the walls it was hot, the breeze could not blow through, and butterflies darted in the tall grass, trapped in the stillness.

No one living could remember when San Sebastián had been a real church, but old people remembered the tale from their parents. San Sebastián, who tended sheep, had had his own church, just as the Patrón, San Juan, had his church. But one day San Sebastián had decided to go away. He gathered his sheep together, and got on his horse. Then his older brother San Juan had come to him, and had invited San Sebastián to come live in his church. But San Sebastián went away and no one cared for his church. At last he came back and now lived with his older brother in the great white church on the plaza.

The policemen stood in the doorway while the Doctor, through Mario, ordered the body unstrapped from the boy and thrown on the one rickety table which still remained in a corner of the ruined building. The scribes did this work quickly, but when the Doctor ordered the tunic and the cotton shirt and pants removed, no one stepped forward. The scribes were mute, as though they did not understand the order when Mario transmitted it in Tzotzil.

Doctor Méndez became impatient, and was not amused by Mario's impotent grin. He told Mario to do the work, and the assistant risked saying this was not his work.

Juan López Oso was holding the rope tied to the killer's arm. Suddenly he jerked it, and ordered the boy to undress his father. Responding like an animal, the boy went to the table, undid the belt and carefully lifted the front of the tunic over his father's face. Then he stepped back.

"Son of God!" the Doctor shouted, and in his anger he

himself yanked the tunic from under the body, took his
scalpel from the pocket of his smock, ripped the front of
the dirty shirt open, and tore it off. For a second he grap-
pled numbly with the drawstrings of the cotton pants.

"Maybe he's trying to screw him," said Oso in Tzotzil
to the scribes standing around him, and everyone laughed.

Still in haste, the Doctor cut the drawers down the side,
and pulled them off. The pants seemed to have been holding the legs down, for once free the knees rose slightly, as
though the murdered man was trying vainly to cover his
private parts.

As a group the scribes and policemen crowded in around
the son to see, and then they were driven back by the
smell.

The corpse was smooth, unsegmented, almost unmarked
by lines of muscle or hair. The skin was the brown of card-
board, except the shins and the arms, which were darker
from the sun.

Wrinkled only in the feet, the upturned face, the hands
and the genitals. There was some statement there, the
Doctor thought as he tested each of the limbs for stiffness.
He turned the body over to look at the smooth back of the
man. Heavy clots of tarnished yellow excrement caked the
legs.

The statement. All the essentials about an Indian are
there in the wrinkled dark parts of his body, the Doctor
said to himself. The Indian's face for eating and talking,
his feet for walking, his hands for working, his cock for
loving or whatever one wants to call it—fucking is probably better.

And his ass for shitting, the Doctor was forced to add
when the smell really reached him. But the ass of the man
was not wrinkled, and this fact ruined the pure truth of

the Doctor's saying. Well, statements are the work of other men, the Doctor decided. Especially statements about Indians.

Finished with the external examination, the Doctor told Mario to go ahead and then he himself made the first incisions—from the neck to the waist, and then another line from the navel to the groin. The scribes crowded in to watch again, as though they had never before seen the Doctor reveal the yellow fatty flesh beneath the skin. The Doctor cut underneath and massaged the flesh back until the breastplate was showing. Meanwhile, Mario was efficiently chopping off great clumps of the gray hair. Then he cut a circle around the head with his knife.

Only the flies seemed interested now. They buzzed around the groin, climbing down between the ridges of the legs. Mario's friend the quizzical little Second Alcalde remained, and the killer, even though Juan López Oso had dropped the rope which held him, and had gone outside.

Once the Doctor glanced up at the boy. Probably, he thought, somewhere behind those downcast eyes that child is having his own hellish atonement.

As soon as Mario was finished his cut, the Doctor pulled the scalp forward so it covered the face. The pulling made a noise like old cloth being ripped. But when the Doctor looked he could not be sure anything he was doing affected the boy.

Méndez searched in his pockets for stronger tools, but discovered Mario had forgotten to provide them. He cursed his assistant under his breath, and searched on the ground for a rock. When he found one, he used it as a hammer with his scalpel as chisel while he did the arduous work of breaking through the ribs. Mario had taken the hacksaw and had begun cutting at the head. The rasping noise filled the church, and when the Doctor looked up he saw the Second Alcalde's little mustache bristled constantly.

"Mario." The Doctor smiled. "You're a regular haircut specialist now, in fact." He rested from the work and wiped sweat off his forehead with the back of his rubber-gloved hand. He laughed to let Mario know this was a joke.

Mario pretended to enjoy his boss's humor, laughed and went back to sawing the skull with renewed effort.

Juan López Oso had found a way to get up on top of the thick walls of the building, and now walked along high above the Doctor. Little pieces of plaster tumbled off the wall as Oso walked, and the Doctor could hear them landing behind him. He tried to pay no attention, and went on with his work.

It was cooler on top of the wall, and Oso sat down above the table and the corpse. From this height he could see the whole valley, the long browned grass pasture which ran to the bottom of the hill, the almost-dry lake behind the Cabildo, the plaza, Jacinto's store and his own. Close by was the graveyard, some of the plots marked with little wooden crosses, some outlined with stones. The policemen and the scribes waited there.

"Ho, boy!" Oso called.

No one at the table below looked up. Oso found a cracked piece of plaster, dislodged it from the wall and skimmed it down so it hit the boy's shoulder. Still the boy did not look up.

"Ho, boy, you know what happens to boys who kill their fathers?"

No answer. But Oso could tell he was irritating the Doctor, for Méndez had paused in his hacking.

"They rot and die in jail, and no one ever goes to the cemetery to clean grass from their graves. Not even their mothers put out food for them, because nobody wants them to come back to visit."

Doctor Méndez looked up at his assistant. "What's Oso saying?" he whispered.

Mario translated into Spanish for the Doctor.

"Ho Mario, don't you know what happens to men who cut up dead men?" Oso laughed.

Mario looked down to his work. His friend the Alcalde stared at the ground. Mario knew what Oso might say, and Oso might be right. But a man has his job, doesn't he, Mario asked himself.

"Juan, leave them alone!" the Doctor called.

"Yes, Doctor," Oso said humbly. He sat still for a minute, kicking against the wall with his feet. Then he found another piece of plaster, and tossed it down, meaning to hit the boy. Instead he hit the body on the leg, and the piece of plaster bounced away.

"Leave us alone!" Méndez shouted. Oso didn't answer.

The Doctor thought of pretending to have found what he was looking for, having the body dumped in the grave, and going back to the Cabildo to write up some false report. But he wondered if doing this would help the boy in any way. Again, he could not tell, and went on hammering through the ríbs with his improvised chisel.

When Mario finished with his hacksaw he signaled the Doctor. The Doctor gripped the slippery bone and tried to wrench it off. There was plenty of dark blood, dribbling onto the ground, and as Méndez pulled the white of the bone showed through where Mario had made his cut.

Up above on the wall, Juan López Oso saw what was

about to happen, stood up and called to the scribes to come in and watch. He himself hurried along the wall to the place where he could get down.

The naked smelly body was forgotten by everyone except the boy, who maintained a solemn dumb watch over it. From experience with other autopsies the scribes knew that here was the important moment, and they looked on the Doctor's work with all the silent intensity of worshipers at a mass.

Mario, embarrassed before his friends over the part he was forced to take, giggled nervously when the Doctor ordered a few extra cuts in the bone to free the bowl of the skull. When at last it was loose the Doctor placed it on the ground, where it was immediately covered with flies. Méndez began to uncover the gray and bloody brain, lifting off the thin skin over it.

Oso pushed into the crowd, bent down and grabbed up the head bowl. He stepped closer to the boy.

"Look!" he said, thrusting the bowl under the boy's nose. "For you to eat out of when you go to jail!" The scribes turned to watch, and Oso bent in close to see the boy's reaction.

There was none.

Oso was angered at this and slammed the bowl against the boy's face. The boy tried to duck away, but he was too slow. Oso grabbed him around the shoulders with one arm, and held him tight.

Even Méndez stopped when he saw it. He could hear the boy's rapid, frantic breathing as it echoed within the skull bowl.

"Enough," said the Doctor, striding up to Oso, with his scalpel still in his rubber-gloved hand.

Oso released his hold on the boy's shivering body, but did not take away the bone.

"Give me that!" Méndez's voice was hard.

Again Oso did not move.

"Give me that!" the Doctor repeated loudly.

"Tell him," said Oso in Tzotzil, without turning from looking into the Doctor's eyes, "tell him it is our custom, and he must not interfere."

The Doctor considered it a sign of weakness in his opponent that he spoke Tzotzil now, since his Spanish was very good.

Mario mumbled a translation of what Oso said.

"Is that true?" the Doctor asked in reply.

Mario did not have to face the Doctor, so he lied. "I don't know."

The Doctor went to Oso calmly, took his hand and pulled it away from the boy's face.

Oso gave in easily. He began laughing when he handed the skull bowl to the Doctor. Then he drifted back to the group of scribes and started talking in a low voice, as though nothing had happened.

The Doctor put the skull bowl back on the ground. "Tell them to get that boy out of here. Let him go dig the grave, or anything," he said. To calm himself he took special care with the membrane, running his fingers under it softly.

Mario repeated the Doctor's message, but no one moved. The boy was left to stand guard beside the body. A little fresh liquid blood painted his nose and chin where the bowl had been.

"Here," Méndez said, looking up like a scholar from his book, "pour some water here." He indicated the membrane.

Mario did not translate.

"You want water?" It was Oso who answered in deep Spanish from the back of the group of scribes.

The Doctor nodded, choosing not to notice it was Oso who responded to his request.

Oso stepped out of the group and got hold of the rope on the boy's arm. He pulled and led the stumbling boy to the end of the table. Like flies frightened away by any movement, the scribes moved back and let Oso bring the boy through.

Oso told him what he was to do in soft tones which might be mistaken for gentleness or encouragement by an outsider. When the boy did not seem to understand, Oso brought the bucket of fresh water, and placed it in the boy's hands.

The Doctor was irritated by Oso's new, more subtle cruelty, but he suppressed his feeling. It was none of his business what the Indians did to one another, he told himself. His job came later. Let them fight, he would bandage them. Let them foolishly expose themselves to sickness, let the Indian curers do what they could to bring back the "soul" of the sick man. When they were through with magic, they could come to him and he would repair what still remained of their wasted bodies.

Let them torture each other. Let Oso torment the boy. The Indian Institute, thought the Doctor, did not pay him to teach humanity. That was the Maestro's work. And a fine job he seemed to be doing, Méndez thought as he pointed to the spot on the membrane he wanted doused with water.

He had become sick, and could not remember why the prospect of this autopsy had seemed almost pleasant earlier in the morning. So he searched the membrane, found a dark spot near the front, and pointed it out to Mario.

"See here? Look. When the head dies first, when it's hit first, this skin grows dark. So we know the son's story is true. The father died from the blows on the head."

Mario nodded sagely, as though he had known all along this was the secret they were searching for. Oso asked him to translate what the Doctor said. When Mario repeated the decision in Tzotzil, the scribes nodded and hummed in agreement.

Even the boy nodded dumbly in affirmation when Mario said he had killed his father with blows on the head.

"We were drunk. I had come home from hot country."

"What's he say?" asked the Doctor quickly.

In Spanish, Mario repeated what the boy had said.

For the hundredth time the Doctor looked at the expressionless, stained face. "Ask him if he loved his father or if he hated him."

Mario only giggled. "I can't," he said.

The Doctor shrugged.

Satisfied that the important part was over, the scribes began to go outside to get the policemen to start digging a grave. Oso pulled on the boy's rope and took him along. The boy was still carrying the pail of water.

An old woman had joined the policemen, who were sitting on the ground passing a cigarette from one to another. The man Salvador, who had not come inside the church, identified her as the wife of the dead man. She avoided her son, did not even look at him, but came to Oso to beg him to give her the body when the Doctor and the officials were through with it. He told her she would

not want the body once the Doctor had finished. She
begged again and again he refused, but he told her she
could stay to see her husband put in the ground.

Oso, still holding the rope, led the boy out to the far
edge of the unshaded, stark grave plot, to the half-finished
row of mounds. The policemen brought shovels, marked
out the size of the hole by scooping off the grass. Then
Oso put the boy to work digging. Somewhere he had
dropped his pail and the remaining water had spilled out.

Left alone, the Doctor went back to work with a haste
which suddenly took on the look of brutality. With the
boy gone, he felt free to act with the dead thing the way
he wanted. He had Mario hold down the shoulders, and
used both hands to force up the chest plate. The head,
capless, hung off the end of the table, and as the Doctor
pulled, blood ran for a steady minute down into the cup
on the ground.

"See here," the Doctor called to Mario, "see how thin
the chest muscles are. Thin but quite strong, tight. And
here"—he fished into the cavity—"the lungs are deflated
now. But look how big they are. Because your people work
their lives away here in the mountains. At high altitudes
you use more air than we do. And here, the heart is bigger
too. Same reason."

The Doctor continued his work, summarily, with little
care any more. From his pocket Mario took surgical
thread, a needle and pliers. With his new-learned skill the
assistant held the skull bowl back in place and pulled the
clipped scalp back over it before he began to sew.

By mistake the Doctor punctured the bloated stomach,
and gas escaped with the sound of air coming from a tire.
"Sorry," said the Doctor to no one, and stepped back so
the smell of the gas wouldn't overcome him.

Soon Mario went outside to get men to carry the body. Some policemen came and to avoid trouble took care of it themselves, without making the boy carry his burden the last bit of the way. They had reclothed the man only in his tunic, and he looked strangely young, like an overgrown schoolboy with his shorn head and shirtless nakedness. The Doctor came out, whistling. There was no washup water left, so the Doctor asked Mario to pull off his rubber gloves. Free of them, the Doctor wiped his sweating, long hands on his white coat, and then lit a cigarette.

Leaving Mario to clean the instruments and the gloves, he walked back to the village alone, again happy with his morning and satisfied with his lot. When he got to town he would go up to her room and shower, and perhaps his Anna would join him under the warm water. He would not tell her about the autopsy. It would only make her more loath than ever to touch his sleek, muscular body. Somewhere they must find a balance in their ideas of the body—between his easy acceptance and her horror. Perhaps if she had seen the man today, she would not attach so much cold sacredness to the human body. No, he decided, it would only increase her terror of her lover's strength, and her fear that his passion was mechanical, devoted to himself rather than to her own slender mind or body. What would she think if she had seen him wrenching that breastplate, or pounding furiously against the resilient, hollow-sounding ribs? It might remind her too much of the Doctor's own fiery, rending brand of love.

She would say I looked like the Devil in Hell trying to steal a soul, the Doctor laughed to himself.

Mario followed the others out to the hole with its pile of dirt banked neatly beside it. Oso still held the leash on the boy, who sat exhausted on the ground, and Oso was arguing with one of the scribes.

"How deep, Mario?" Oso called out.

"To his own height," Mario said.

"There. I'm right," said the scribe who had been arguing with Oso.

"This is deep enough," Oso proclaimed, pointing again at the squared-off hole. "The dogs won't get to him in there. That's what it's for."

Several others looked into the hole and agreed with Oso. So they unceremoniously dumped the body inside. The dead man fell on his back, his tunic pulled off to one side, revealing the thick line where the Doctor had carelessly sewn over his incisions. The old woman got up, crying, to look in, but the policemen had already begun replacing the dirt. Quickly all joined in, shoveling with their hands and with sticks. The mound was made and Oso stood on top, pounding it down with his feet. The scribes and the policemen began to leave for their midday meals.

Oso thought about his brother Miguel. Miguel worked now for a Mexican named Don Alonso on a fruit farm which lay on the border of Chomtik near San Martín. Coming home this morning, Oso had Jacinto stop the truck and went to see Miguel. Miguel was surprised his brother had come back from Flores. "What for?" he asked. "Why didn't you get work there?" And Oso had been unable to answer his brother.

Going home to his own meal, pleased with the day's fun, Juan López Oso grinned. He was glad he had returned to this place at least for a while.

7 Mario

THE MAESTRO WAS FROM
the city, and when he had first come to Chomtik, he had
found the place static. Though there was his work at the
school, days dragged for him, each one the same.

Turning and looking back toward the village now, he
knew his own eyes had been to blame. In Oaxaca where
he was born, and in Mexico City where he had studied, he
was accustomed to the glittering pageants of progress.
Here he must only watch more carefully.

The Center had not changed today. The buildings—the
mud-walled stores, the Cabildo, the church, all bathed in
pale yellow light from the west and crossed with thick
shafts of shadow—they were the same. But closer, below
him lay the deserted church of San Sebastián. In front of
the church was the graveyard, where they had buried the
murdered man after the autopsy. The Maestro could pick
out the red earth mound which he supposed was the new
grave. Two women were following their sheep home
through the cemetery, letting the animals graze briefly on
the grass-covered plots, swatting lambs with the long
sticks they carried for herding.

Mario had been waiting impatiently for the Maestro for
over an hour. He was in some hurry to get home, so the
Maestro followed him up over the hill, and they started
down into the next valley at a fast clip, Mario's sandals
marking a steady thump on the path. They passed between walls made of sod and topped with bushes. A man
and his son, both hatless, worked clearing stubble off a

plot of land they would plant in April. They looked up
from behind the wall and called to Mario, "Brother!"

"Brother!" Mario called back.

All the land was dry these days, the pastures brown,
and the cornstalks bent over and dead.

When the Maestro had first arrived, during the rainy
season in the preceding summer, it had all seemed ugly
and barren to him. The constant variation of light on the
hills was interesting enough, but the shrubbery was thin
and deep red gashes of erosion scarred every hillside.

Then the Maestro had decided to learn what he could
about the place, and began going home with Mario to
spend the night from time to time. Now, though it was
the dry season, the Maestro saw what was before him as
a rich place, populated in a hundred ways. If he listened
carefully he could hear an unseen person calling another
over the wind. Or dogs barking, or roosters confused into
crowing by the sunset.

The two men turned off onto a narrower path. Soon
they passed a house where men stood out in the front
yard. Inside someone was playing harp and another man
guitar, the unending monotony of the song of San Juan.
Mario barely looked up, but the Maestro stopped. The
men in the yard were drunk and took no notice of him. As
he watched people began to come from the house, and at
last a group of men carried out a white pine box. The
women who came last were crying, and their shouts mixed
with the music of the harp and guitar.

The burial party passed out the front gate of the house,
and Mario took off his hat. No one seemed to notice the
Maestro or the Doctor's helper. One man, very drunk, sat
down suddenly almost at the Maestro's feet. The rest of
the people were already well up the trail, and the drunk's

woman, her hair hanging about her face, got a hold on her husband's arm, and tried to pull him to his feet. Two younger girls, probably daughters, stood watching.

Mario spoke in a low quick voice to the woman, and then took the Maestro's arm and led him on, away from the scene.

"What happened?" asked the Maestro.

"They went to bury that man's brother, and he's very drunk and very sad in his heart."

"How did the man die?"

"I don't know, I wasn't there."

Mario led the way. It was colder, the sun had gone, and soon they reached the house of Mario's father, which was hidden almost completely by trees.

There was nothing here, the Maestro thought, that wasn't here before the Spaniards came four hundred years ago. The walls of the house were mud plastered into sticks. The roof was a pyramid of thatch twice as tall as the rest of the house. Smoke seeped out under the eaves and through the thatch. Two thin dogs, one tan, the other black, came running to bark at Mario and the Maestro as they ducked through the place in the shrub fence which was the gate of the sitio.

Mario's mother, a wall-eyed old woman of great assurance, heaviness and laughter, was sitting in the doorway, spinning thread onto a stick from a tuft of wool she held in her other hand. She greeted them, and told her son that his father had had a good day. In the morning the sick man had felt well enough to get up for a while. Now he was tired and lay on the wooden bed inside the house, curled up under blankets. Mario and the Maestro went inside and found the old man with his head turned to the wall. He was stroking a gray cat. He turned and smiled at them, a wrinkled old smile, and then he bid the Maestro good evening in Spanish. Ten years before when he had been President of Chomtik he had known enough Spanish to deal with Don Roberto and the other government men in San Martín, but since then, especially since he had been sick, he had forgotten much of it.

Mario went to the bed and bent down. "I've come, Father," he whispered.

His father reached out a thin hand and touched his boy lightly on the head. "Good."

"I saw the curer, Father, and he's going to come to you the day after tomorrow."

The father nodded his head and smiled.

Mario's mother asked him if he wanted some corn gruel, if he and the Ladino were hungry, but Mario explained it was late and they should be getting to his house. The old woman nodded, and Mario took his visitor outside.

His son Pascual, who was a first grade student at the Maestro's school, was waiting for him in the yard. The two men ducked out under the fence, the son followed, and as they crossed down to the road, the boy broke into a run toward his own house.

"Look there," said Mario in Spanish, pointing down the valley. "You can see Don Alonso's orchards."

Below them, beyond Mario's tight little sitio, was another piece of land, and beyond that a fence and then several large fields of fruit trees, set in a pocket of land at the bottom of the valley. This was the end of Chomtik, the beginning of Mexican land owned by the richest man in San Martín. Seeing those even rows of trees, bare at this time of year, the Maestro longed to have the power to take all this from Don Alonso and give it to Mario. It was a bitter feeling he had, but it passed quickly enough

when he told himself this was the way the world was and
would have to remain, at least for the moment.

Pascual's little legs carried him home just quickly
enough, for Mario and the Maestro were at the front gate
by the time Pascual had run inside and told his mother
they were coming.

"I've come," the Maestro called out from the gate.

The woman came to the low doorway brushing corn
dough from her big hands onto her skirt.

"You've come," she answered him in Tzotzil, smiling.

The Maestro followed his host inside the gate, and
looked into the small sheep pen made of boards. It was
empty. Probably, he thought, Mario's two oldest children,
Antun and Lupa, were out herding Mario's two sheep.

"Where did your sheep go?" the Maestro asked Mario's
woman in Tzotzil.

Maruch kept a straight face. "They died."

"No!" he said in mock surprise, "it's not so!"

"Yes," she said firmly, adjusting the shawl which held
her sleeping baby on her back.

"No."

Maruch gave in easily with a shrug. "The children will
bring them home in a little while." She laughed and the
Maestro laughed as though he was relieved.

"What's going on there with the baby?" he asked, since
the first question had provoked such amusement.

Maruch became all somber again. "She died."

"No!" said the Maestro in shock, and then they all had a
big laugh, since the baby woke up at that moment and
demanded her mother's breast with little belching cries.

They went inside the house, which was the same as
Mario's father's but smaller, and Maruch returned to her
work beside the fire in the middle of the dirt floor. Flames

blazed around a blackened kettle which held the greens cooking for supper, but it seemed dark inside, and it took a minute for their eyes to adjust. Mario produced his one tiny chair for the Maestro and then sat on the edge of the board bed. Pascual came to stand by his father's knee, staring into the fire and catching his breath from his run up the hill to the house. The youngest son, Manvel, sat by the fire, his hair a messy tangle, his face and uncinched tunic filthy. He smiled at the Maestro and imitated his mother. "You've come."

The Maestro assured the little boy that he had come.

The baby slept fitfully, wrapped in a shawl and tied to her mother's back, rocking with the movement of her mother as Maruch ground corn between her mano and metate—a stone rolling pin against a stone trough on the floor.

The fire made the room warm and smoky and Mario rested from the walk home with his eyes shut. The smoke made the Maestro's eyes run.

Maruch stopped her work to poke at the boiling greens with her fingers. "Do you know how to eat turnip greens?" she asked.

It was an idle question, since the Maestro had eaten turnip leaves before in this house, but he told her he knew how and that he thought they were good.

Because she was no longer being rocked by her mother's movement, the baby woke up with a start, very cross, and began to cry. No one paid any attention, so she cried louder.

Maruch decided the greens were done and lifted the heavy pot off the fire. She took her comal, a heavy platter cut from an old oil drum, and placed it carefully over the flames. On this griddle she would cook the tortillas after she patted the corn dough into thin round cakes. She took a low stool from the corner, switched the crying baby around so the child could reach her breast, and began patting the first of the tortillas on the stool. She touched the griddle lightly, it was warm enough, so she flipped the tortilla into place for cooking.

Fifty to sixty pats a tortilla, twenty-five to thirty tortillas in the morning for her family, the same number at night, Maruch gave three thousand, three hundred thumps to that stool every day, thought the Maestro.

While working, she asked Mario something about the day just past, speaking too fast for the Maestro to understand. But the Maestro was able to catch the name of Juan López Oso, and took the opportunity to ask Mario about him.

"Did you say Juan López Oso has a new woman?"

"Yes."

"Did his old wife die?" the Maestro asked.

Mario was amused when he said no.

"Then he has two wives. Do many men have two?"

"If they can afford it, some do," Mario said.

"But you don't."

"No, I can't afford it."

"But you work for the Institute, you make good money."

Mario agreed to this, but added he had to help support his father. The Maestro was sure there was still another reason.

"What would Maruch think if you brought home another wife?"

Maruch had been watching their conversation in Spanish very carefully, so when Mario turned and put the question to her, she broke out laughing.

"If he came with another woman I'd take my pot and

my children and go back to my mother's house." She said it without rancor, and even the children in question, especially Pascual, laughed.

"You," she went on, still patting a tortilla, "how many women do you have?"

"No wife yet," said the Maestro, thinking of Carla waiting a lonely night for him in the teachers' quarters.

Maruch nodded. "But you do know how to sleep with a woman?"

The Maestro assured her that he did, and she laughed some more.

"It's better to have a woman," said Maruch, looking up at him. "Less cold at night when you're sleeping."

The Maestro agreed it was better, and then looked to Mario. Mario smiled, though he had been thinking of the warning his friend the Second Alcalde had given him in the morning.

"You don't like this Juan López Oso, do you?" the Maestro asked Mario.

"There's nothing wrong with him."

"But why don't you like him?"

Mario thought a moment, pressing his folded hands together between his knees. "Do you know what our word *chanul* means?" he said finally.

"Of course," the Maestro said. "That's your word for soul."

"But I don't think it's the same thing," Mario said. "A man's *chanul* is the animal he has. Some men have sheep and others have cows or pigs. A man told me once my soul is a rabbit, but who knows if that's true."

Mario breathed and looked into the fire. He found it difficult and dangerous to say what he had to say now to the Maestro. "And some men, when they're drunk, they tell you what animal they have. This Juan López Oso was drunk once, and he told me his animal is a tiger." Mario laughed. "I don't know whether to believe it. But a man knows best about himself."

"It's true," the Maestro said, "Oso's a strong man. But don't you see, that's what your village needs."

"Maybe," said Mario. "But Oso is dangerous too. He makes me afraid."

The Maestro laughed. "But he's your neighbor, isn't he?"

"Yes, his land is right over there."

"And you're friends?"

"Yes, I think so."

Mario stretched his feet closer to the fire, and rested his hand on Pascual's head. The boy was exhausted from his walk to and from school, and had dropped off to sleep sitting with his back against his father's bed.

In a while, the baby, satiated, gave up her mother's breast and went to sleep in her lap. It was almost an hour before Maruch whispered to Mario and he asked the Maestro if he was ready to eat.

Then Mario went outside in the cold and brought in a low table which he placed between the Maestro and himself, carefully adjusting it so the legs sat evenly on the dirt floor.

"Where did Antun and Lupa go?" he asked his wife.

"I don't know. They went to watch the sheep, and Antun was looking for firewood."

"It's late now."

She nodded and passed the two men a gourd bowl of water so they could wash their mouths and their hands. After rinsing his mouth, the Maestro spat toward the fire, as he had learned to do from Mario. The woman next passed a bowl of greens, which Mario put down on the table, and a flat dish of tortillas, the top one still steaming, since Maruch had just plucked it off the comal. Mario sprinkled some rough-grained salt over the greens and then stirred the bowl with his finger.

"Eat," he told the Maestro in Tzotzil.

"I'm going to, thank you," said the Maestro.

He took one of the white tortillas, and pulled it in two. Then Mario took the other half. Each tore off a triangular piece and doubled it in his right hand, making a sort of crude spoon to take up a piece of the greens.

Maruch woke Pascual and Manvel and pushed a bowl of greens between them. Manvel cried when he woke up and did not stop until he began eating.

There were noises outside, children talking. Mario laid his tortilla on the table, and cracked the door a bit, letting the smoke blow toward his wife and baby, and the cold air streamed across the fire. In the dark outside he could hear his daughter pushing the two sheep into their pen by the gate. The girl pressed herself between the doors and came in chattering from the cold. She went immediately and sat beside her mother. The girl did not look up at the Maestro.

"Cold," she whispered to her mother.

"Where were you?" Maruch asked, continuing to pat the dough on the stool.

The girl did not answer.

Antun, the oldest son, had come home with his sister, loaded down with sticks. He stacked some against the mud wall under the eaves and brought the rest inside and dropped them near the fire. The boy also went to the Maestro's school, and when the Maestro said hello to him, he smiled but did not speak. Unlike his brother Pascual,

Antun was old enough for pants, but his father had not yet bought them, so Antun made do with his tunic, carefully tucking it between his legs before he sat down by the fire to warm himself.

Mario and the Maestro went on eating, and the boy's mother passed Antun three or four tortillas, and he began dipping into the bowl with his younger brothers at once.

"Where were you?" Mario asked his son.

Antun spoke between mouthfuls. "We were with the sheep, there on Juan López Oso's land, and then we went to look for wood. When we came back the sheep were gone, and we went looking for them. Down there by the fence into the rancho, we found two Mexican men, and they had the sheep. We asked for them to give them back, and they said the sheep weren't ours. One of them was Oso's brother who wears the Mexican clothes, and finally he let me bring the sheep home."

The boy continued eating.

"Where were they?" the Maestro asked Mario in Spanish.

"They got lost in the dark," Mario said.

The food was not tasty for the Maestro, but he found it warm and filling. When he had finished he sat back and thanked Maruch, who by now had finished making tortillas and was eating herself, sharing a bowl with the oldest girl.

She took a small pot of water off the fire, and got out a block of caked brown sugar. Lupa passed her a machete which stood against the wall, and she chopped off a lump of the sugar, dropped it in the pot and stirred it. In a minute she handed the Maestro and Mario cups of this "coffee" as the Indians called it. Sweet water to the Maestro, but at least hot.

When he had finished Mario leaned back on the bed. The youngest children were asleep by the dying fire. Mario could hear the wind whipping around the house.

"*Ik'aletik,*" he said, opening his eyes and looking at the Maestro.

"What's that mean?" the Maestro asked.

"People say there are little men who come down from the mountains in the night, and fly around our houses. If we aren't watching carefully they take our women off to the mountains and rape them. But who knows if it's true." Mario laughed, self-consciously.

The Maestro laughed, to show he did not believe these stories.

"You know," Mario said, "when my other sheep were taken at first I thought I heard the *ik'al* outside."

"When was it?" the Maestro asked, opening his eyes and peering at his friend through the heavy wood smoke.

"That was last year—I had five sheep then. I was here in my house—it was before I went to work for the Doctor. It was winter, cold like this. But already February—it was the first day of the fiesta at Carnaval. In the night we were sleeping, and my wife said there was someone outside. '*Ik'al,*' I said.

"But then I thought it was a man. At first I thought Juan López Oso. His house is here close by, and in a dream once he had come to steal sheep from me.

"Then I knew it was coyotes. They come here from hot country when it is winter there and they find nothing to eat. And they take our sheep.

"I heard the sounds and then it was at the gate there," Mario went on. "When I got outside they had climbed over the pen, and torn out the boards, and taken one of the white sheep. The coyotes were quiet, quieter than dogs. They come here, eight or ten of them and you can't tell they have come until after they kill the sheep. Then they make noise. They had dragged my white sheep down to the road there, and eaten at her throat, so there was blood and she was dead. I found her in the road with blood at her throat, and I shot at the coyotes with my gun, but there were too many of them.

"I went across to my father's house, and my father came with his gun, and my younger brother Mateo came too. My wife was afraid and put wood on the fire to make a bright light when I was gone, but I wasn't afraid myself when my father and my brother came. We were looking for the coyotes over the hill on Oso's land then. There was a moon and a lot of light, and we could see them, too far away to shoot, at the top of the hill.

"So we were looking for them all over, in the gullies, because they hide in the gullies. While we were out looking they came back and took two more of the sheep. My wife and my son Antun tried to stop them, to frighten them with burning sticks, but the coyotes weren't afraid.

"They got away with the two more sheep, and took them out to the road and ate at their throats and killed them. They weren't hungry, they only wanted to kill. That's why I looked for them with my gun, and with my brother Mateo looking too, and all night we were on the hills. The coyotes ran away to the mountains when the sun came, but we went out looking and missed the fiesta, because we searched for them the next day, and the next night too."

"Then what?" the Maestro asked. He could not be sure, but it seemed that Mario was distressed by this memory.

He talked with his eyes shut against the smoke, and his face was contorted.

"And then nothing happened. I had lost my three sheep, and I couldn't have a new tunic this year. That's all. And I was sad about it, but more I had bad thoughts about the coyotes, and thought about them at night when I was sleeping, because they killed the sheep without wanting to eat them. That's all."

Mario's face straightened, and he opened his eyes to the Maestro, and he smiled. He was wiping out the bad memory himself, and did not want the Maestro to be sad with him.

Maruch asked her husband what they had been talking about, although she already had a good idea. When he told her she stopped, took her hand off the sleeping baby's head and stared into the fire.

"Do you want to sleep?" asked Mario.

"Yes."

Mario took out two old pieces of burlap, and laid them on the floor by the fire. On top of this he put one of the wool blankets from his bed. Again he asked the Maestro if he did not want the bed to sleep on, and again the Maestro refused.

Mario picked up the two youngest boys and put them, still asleep, in the middle of the bed. Maruch, after putting a jar of corn on the embers of the fire to cook for the next morning, got up with the baby in her arms and climbed over the sleeping boys to the back corner of the bed. Mario stretched in the firelight, unbuckled his tunic, lifted it over his head and rolled it up to use as a pillow. When he lay down on the outside of the bed, Maruch spread the remaining blanket over him and the children.

Antun and Lupa slept on the dirt floor at the foot of their parents' bed.

"Maestro?" asked Mario. "Are you happy in your heart?"

"Yes," answered the other.

"Good."

"Until tomorrow, Mario."

The Maestro was half asleep when Mario, invisible now the fire was only a few red eyes, called again.

"Maestro?"

"Yes?"

"Do you hear that?"

The Maestro heard only the wind whipping around the corners of the house, whistling through the thatch.

"Yes. Is that *ik'al*?"

"That's the dead people seeing if we're well, if we have our souls, and are warm."

"Oh, good." The Maestro was sleepy.

"Protecting me from the Doctor."

"Oh."

"Until tomorrow," said Mario, giggling.

8   The President

AFTER DARK, BUT BEFORE his meal was ready, the President came out of his house, and crossed the plaza. First he went to the house of the little Second Alcalde, Mario's friend.

When the President called, the man came, not from inside, but from behind the house, rearranging his clothes, running his outsized hands through his hair. He invited the President to come in, and offered him a drink, which the President refused. The man's wife was frightened by the President, stopped her corn grinding and sat still in a corner of the large, drafty, almost empty room.

The President knew this man had served a short term in the jail of Santo Domingo, though he did not know what for. When the little man with his bushy eyebrows and mustache came to the Cabildo to do his job hearing cases, he brought fiber and a piece of leather. Strapping the leather to his thigh he sat all day listening while he rolled the fiber against the leather to make cord. He was always busy with his hands. Now unoccupied, while the President cleared his throat and spat toward the fire, the hands fluttered about their owner, picking at dirt on the floor, scratching his legs, smoothing down the wrinkled cuffs of his dirty pants.

The President stated as a fact that the Second Alcalde knew how to make net bags, good ones. Bags for women to carry charcoal, or pots. Bags for a man who couldn't afford a leather bag. Bags school children used. Good ones. Although perhaps a little frightened himself by the important visitor, the Second Alcalde agreed with pride that he did know how to make bags—good ones. Politely, the President asked what the man got for each bag he sold. The man did not believe he could possibly have a customer, but gave the asking price—twelve pesos for the big bag with the red and green sewing at the top.

"Man," said the President slowly, "there is a boy going to Santo Domingo tomorrow—"

"I know, President." The Second Alcalde's head wagged up and down. His hands were suddenly dead, clasped together in his lap.

"To live there," continued the President. "Will you teach him this?" He pointed at an almost-finished white bag lying beside the Second Alcalde's chair.

The wife looked over quickly. It was a strange request, and the President had been thinking since noon, pondering whether he could ask this favor of the Second Alcade.

"When, President?" One of the man's hands, the right one, escaped and reached for the bag. His eyebrows were up, and his mustache jumping, as though he were chewing the President's request.

"Tonight. If he doesn't learn tonight, and a man cannot learn to make such fine bags in a night, you go to Santo Domingo as his friend, you teach him there."

It was a big request, and the man naturally would want to think it over. He looked to his wife, asking her with his wide-open eyes and raised eyebrows if he dare beg the President to pay him for the work. But his wife gave no clue, and the President had become impatient and nervous again.

"Yes, President. Gladly, President."

"Good." The great man stood up. "Here," he said, reaching into his shirt pocket. "This will pay for your trips to town, to the jail." He gave the little craftsman a dirty ten-peso bill, and they shook hands. The Second Alcalde could not hide his pleasure and his scraggly mustache spread as the grin widened on his face.

Outside again in the still night, the President was relieved. He felt a great and lasting burden of duty to the boy had been taken away.

How weird his coming and his request must have seemed to the Second Alcalde. A man gives his craft to his son, the same natural way he teaches the boy to farm corn, without thinking about it. Teaches, thought the President as he crossed the gully by the road and ducked under the fence. But what does a teacher give his son? Nothing more than he gives to the sons of other men.

The President had wanted his eldest son, his Eliseo, to be special somehow. And perhaps he was. Eliseo was only eighteen, and already he made good money running Jacinto's store. He spoke Spanish as well as his father, and did not fear the Ladinos in town. He knew how to deal with them.

But it was hard for the President to say if the boy was special. They did not see each other as much any more, since Jacinto had become Eliseo's great friend. The boy spent most of his time in the store, in the evening he ate with Jacinto, and maybe drank with him too. Sometimes they would come to the President's house together to listen to the President's radio. But they only listened, staring at the floor, avoiding the tentative bits of conversation the President threw to them.

At those times the President wished Jacinto would go away, and there would be an excuse to turn off the radio. When Eliseo was younger, after his mother died, they had talked a great deal together. Though the boy did not really understand about Mexico City, he was eager to hear about it. In those days, when he still lived with his father, the boy had a natural kind of grace, a keen kind of expectation on his face, and the President looked forward to a time when their talk would be real talk, between two knowing men.

But Eliseo left when the President got a new woman. Not in anger, since he knew his father needed someone to cook and care for his house. He told his father the day he took his things to Jacinto's store that with the new woman his father would need more space. The woman had her own children, and Eliseo said it was not good for her to have to make food for so many people, so many tortillas, and he could take his meals from Jacinto's young wife.

Outside the door of Jacinto's, the President paused. There were low voices inside. He rapped and was admitted by Eliseo. Two scribes were drinking town brandy at the lone table under the gas lamp and they rose when the President came in. Jacinto and Eliseo were at the counter together, poring over a picture magazine Jacinto had brought from town. The little room was warm and well-lit, and in the back Jacinto's wife was praying softly before a row of candles. Her baby, blessed with Jacinto's moon face, lay in her lap, one hand inside her blouse.

The two scribes were drunk, and excused themselves and left. The President took one of the seats.

"Jacinto?"

"Yes, President? What do you say?" Jacinto spoke in Spanish, with a light tone. Through marriage the President was his uncle, and the younger man had no awe for him.

"Tomorrow I have to go to San Martín with the boy, to see Don Roberto, and go to the court. Can we go early in the truck?"

"What time, President?"

"At six?"

Jacinto laughed and Eliseo smiled.

"Oh, I think not, Uncle, I think not. Too early. Why not when I go as usual at seven-thirty?"

"All right, that will do." The President gave up his carefully worked out plan for the next day.

"You won't have some brandy, Uncle?" Jacinto asked, almost as an apology.

"No, thank you."

"But it's all right that we take a little?" Jacinto jerked his head in Eliseo's direction as though he were really asking the father's permission.

"Of course," said Eliseo, embarrassed. "He doesn't care."

Jacinto poured two small glasses of the brandy.

"A soft drink, Uncle?" Jacinto offered. "Will you have a Pepsi-Cola?"

"No, thank you." The President could not decide whether he really wanted it or not. "I'll sit here a minute."

"Good, President. Good. Will you have something to eat, some meat and tortillas?"

The President shook his head—no, he had to go home soon. The two boys drank in silence, and the President wished Jacinto would not play the good-natured host with him.

Eliseo answered a knock at the door, letting in Juan López Oso. Oso shrugged off the drink Jacinto offered him, and took the other seat at the table with the President. From inside his tunic he took a small black radio and turned it on.

"This is the voice of Flores, music for the *whole* state of Chiapas!" the exuberant broadcaster shouted. "When the waitress brings you beer, tell her—" and singing followed.

> *Pardon me, Pardon me,*
> *But I drink Corona. . . .*

"Yes," the voice said, "wherever you go, let them know Corona is your beer!"

Jacinto moved to the table to admire the new radio.

"Do you like it, President?" asked Oso, smiling and showing his gold teeth in his pride.

"Yes." The sound was better than on his own radio, thought the President.

"Three hundred pesos. It cost me three hundred pesos in Flores. The best radio they have there."

"It's good," said Eliseo, nodding his head in agreement.

"Come listen to it in my store, whenever you want," said Oso, rather grandly. "You too, President."

"I have my own radio," said the President, smiling. Then he stood and stretched. "My meal is ready at home."

"Here, President, sit down." Oso pointed at the seat. "Jacinto, bring me two Pepsi-Colas."

Jacinto brought the drinks and the President sat down again. The soft drinks were not cool, but they were sweet, and the President found it helped his hunger.

"President," said Oso, in a low voice, "I have to talk to you about something."

"What?" The President frowned.

Oso knew he had the President's attention now, so he turned off the radio. Jacinto and Eliseo had returned to the counter and the picture magazine.

"There is a man, President, named Salvador, who brought the body of the murdered man from Cruztik yesterday. He has been named a Gobernador this year—"

"Yes," said the President, impatiently, "I talked to him." The President could barely remember the face of the man Salvador, the night before had all the qualities of a dream in his mind. Perhaps, he thought, the man Salvador had come toward morning, after the President dreamed of his wife and the cornstalks cracking in the high wind, and the smoky blue pool where the school children had bathed.

"He doesn't have the money, President. We made a mistake when we put his name on the list."

"We made a mistake, did we?" asked the President, more to himself than to Oso. "Yes, we made a mistake. But how could we have known that this man's sister was the new wife of Juan López Oso? You never told us that."

Jacinto and Eliseo were listening closely, and smirked while the President laughed. Oso did not laugh.

"Well," said the President, "what do you want me to do? Go to the Cabildo and scratch his name off the list?"

He had finished his soft drink and stood up again to stretch.

"Yes, President."

Jacinto whistled under his breath.

"No," said the President calmly.

"But President—"

"I said no."

Oso reached to his face and ran his hand over his whiskers. With his long sharp nails he tried to pluck out an especially long hair, but it would not come.

"Are you angry, President?" he asked, not looking up.

"No, I don't get angry. I have to go home to eat."

Oso nodded, still avoiding the President's gaze.

"Thank you for the drink," the President said, and Oso nodded again, gravely. "At seven-thirty, then?" The President looked to Jacinto and Jacinto nodded in agreement.

"Do you want to come eat?" he asked Eliseo, who seemed to be hiding behind his friend. "I have meat from San Martín."

"No, Father, thank you. My meal is ready here."

"All right."

It was cold outside, silent except for the whip of the wind sweeping down into the valley, and dead, except for a single figure crossing toward the jail, moving like an ant with food, except he had no food, only a tiny flicker of kerosene flame in a lamp he was hiding from the wind.

Good, thought the President, and he almost went across the plaza to thank the little Second Alcalde again, but then he thought better of it. Leave the craftsman and the boy alone.

At the four corners of the plaza were stands of crosses, and by one the President stopped and looked up. The crosses were tall, almost twice his height, made of boards which were gray and rough with age. Arms tilted down, the crosses leaned. The President stopped and looked back across the expanse of the square.

He had been standing here, where a man had set up a liquor stall for the fiesta of Carnaval that February. The President, just Maestro from Cruztik then, was drinking with the man who was Eliseo's godfather. A good man, he lived near the President's home in Lumtik. Later, four or five years, the man started drinking all the time, alone even, and in six months he died. But still, he was a good man, he never fought with anyone, and he always had small coins, ten- or twenty-centavo pieces, to give his godson Eliseo to buy candy.

It was the high day of the fiesta, the day they led out bulls and the men and boys chased them. The women scattered, or sat together near the stores and the Cabildo, laughing at their men, laughing because it was the great fiesta of the year and there was a band of music and a huge market, and skyrockets, and no one could escape the excitement of it. The joy of Carnaval spread up from the young, beginning the first day with the schoolboys, who ran between the market stands like a pack of dogs after a rabbit. And then the joy spread to the young men, the unmarried ones who got drunk together and passed out, slept on the cold ground and then got up and drank again. Finally the joy struck the old men, those too tired to chase the bulls. It struck them last, and perhaps more deeply. In the church, or during the processions of the banners, or when they met a friend from another hamlet they had heard was dead. And here he was, drunk and alive.

They were like crazy dogs, all the men and boys, the young chasing the bulls, the old snorting with pleasure like old dogs asleep in the sun and dreaming.

Eliseo was with his father and godfather that day, holding his godfather's hard hand, and eating sweet hot roasted maguey, while all three watched the swarm of men after the bulls. Eliseo was ten that year, quick-eyed and alert. His father had such pride in him he had taken the boy to Cruztik, to live in the schoolhouse. His wife had not wanted the boy to go so far away, but Eliseo pleaded to be allowed to live with his father. It had been a good year for both of them and the fiesta was fine.

"Was my wife to come today, do you know?" the President had asked Eliseo's godfather.

"I was in Lumtik yesterday. I saw your woman, she said she was sick, but she will try to come here today."

"It doesn't matter," the President said. "We are going home tomorrow to see her."

"Not staying for the end of Carnaval?"

"No." The President smiled. "The last day is always bad, and I think it will rain. Here, drink this," and he poured another glass for the godfather. While they were drinking, Eliseo went away again to search through the crowds of black-dressed women for his mother, and the President thought perhaps he would go to Lumtik that evening, since she was sick and might not come today. When he

and the godfather had finished the bottle they went to the
market stalls and the President bought dried shrimp,
wrapped in newspaper, to take to his wife. It was a delicacy she enjoyed.

Still with the godfather, he returned to the foot of the
crosses, where Eliseo was waiting for them, holding Juan
López Oso's hand. There were tears on the boy's face, and
for once Oso was not smiling and showing his gold teeth.

"You didn't find her?"

The boy shook his head.

"Maestro," said Oso, slowly, "I was looking for you." Oso
cleared his throat, and then had to speak louder, since a
record player in one of the stores near them had begun a
tune. "Maestro, I was coming here this morning, early,
before sunrise, and on the path through Lumtik they told
me your woman was dead. I went to your house but they
had already taken her to her father's house. I did not go
there, but came on to the fiesta to look for you."

Eliseo, who had already heard this, left Oso, and hid
his face against the round chest of his godfather.

"Maestro, will you have a drink?" asked the godfather.

The President was looking at the ground, and nodded.
Oso bought the liquor, a large bottle, and they drank
together. Then, as the President remembered it, they got
candles and went to the church to light them before the
image of the Patrón San Juan. The church was almost
empty, but thick with the smell of incense which had been
burned during the fiesta, and with the smell of the pine
needles which covered the floor.

Someone, perhaps the godfather, had asked him if he
wanted to go home to Lumtik and they had been on their
way out of the church when they met some religious men,
going about the duties of changing the vestments of one

of the wooden saints. Liquor was offered and taken. After
that the President remembered little, except that he lost
Eliseo somewhere, and during the night, or maybe the
following night, it was his own schoolboys from Cruztik
who took him back there. On the trail through the mountains he protested, explaining to them as he stumbled
along that he had to go to Lumtik. No, they told him, he
lived in Cruztik now, and they were going home. He told
the boys that his wife was dead, and they did not believe
him. Come on, Maestro. Be careful there, watch the stones,
Maestro! Careful, Maestro.

So still was the plaza now as the President watched,
that the image of Carnaval that year and the terrible news
faded, leaving him with the sense that the whole thing had
been a dream, like the visit of Salvador the night before.
Though he was quite hungry and his insides grumbled,
the President could not go home. Instead he went to the
dark church, where memories, it seemed, were more
shielded. Untouched by the wind, the smells of pine and
incense lingered in the church, and the President retraced
his steps to the altar rail where he had lit the candle for
his dead wife, and he stood gazing at San Juan, waxen faced
and suffering, for a long time. He watched, not with any
piety, but with a kind of remembered and painful excitement which ran from his stomach to his chest and his heart.

9 Juan López Oso

In Jacinto's store, Oso
paid for the soft drinks, but took as a gift the two drinks
of brandy which the boys had given him. He smoked a
cigarette and thought. Then, with no ceremony, barely

muttering good-by, he took his new radio and left. Next door, in his own place, he found his new woman already asleep, and the fire almost dead. He put the radio away, and took the flashlight he had bought in Flores, and went quickly across the plaza to Don Concepción's house behind the Cabildo.

"Don Concepción?"

"I'm sorry," said Don Concepción's wife in Spanish from inside. "There are no more tortillas, the girl teacher at the school got them all this evening."

"No," explained Oso patiently, "I am to get the keys to the Cabildo office, to find a paper the President wants brought to him."

Don Concepción himself came to the door, hiking up his baggy pants and looking doubtful, but when he saw it was Oso standing in the dark, he passed out his own key ring, and asked if Oso needed a flashlight or a candle.

Oso said no, and took the key ring, wishing Don Concepción a good night's sleep.

While he was opening the Cabildo door, Oso heard gentle talking by the jail. So he stopped, went to the corner, and looked down the long dark porch. There was someone standing there with a feeble light, talking to the boy. Probably a friend or brother who had brought the boy his supper and maybe a bottle of liquor, or who had come to ask why he had done it. For a moment Oso thought of going there and baiting the boy again, but he decided instead to finish his own work at the Cabildo quickly.

The flashlight lit the room enough for him to see, and for the Mexican heroes on the wall to see him. Don Concepción's wall clock would strike the hour nine before he was finished, and Oso remembered not to be frightened when that happened.

A little key opened Don Concepción's desk. Oso put the flashlight down, and in one of the drawers found a stack of papers which the Secretary had typed: the list of Gobernadors for the current year lay buried under the lists of the other officials for the year, Alcaldes, Mayores, Síndicos. Several names had been scratched out already, men who had died, or who had gone to live somewhere else. No one would notice Salvador's name being crossed out, replaced with the name of a neighbor of his in Cruztik. A name which Salvador had given Oso.

Oso found a pencil and blacked out Salvador's name carefully. Beside it he wrote the name of the neighbor. He straightened the pile of papers, and was putting them back in the drawer.

"What are you looking for?" asked the President, who was standing in the doorway.

"My watch, President. I left it here before I went away to Flores."

"I see." The President walked across the room and took the sheaf of papers out of Oso's hand. "Write the man Salvador's name again, in the right place."

"Yes, President," said Oso, smiling like a bad boy with three gold teeth. "Wouldn't it be better to wait until morning? I will have Don Concepción type the list again."

"No," the President said. "I don't want to explain to Don Concepción."

Oso began to work.

He was only ten or twelve years younger than the President. About forty. But the President had now the strange and impossible idea that Oso had been one of his pupils. One of those who turned out badly. Perhaps like the murderer now in the jail.

"Are you angry?"

The President didn't answer.

"I said, Are you angry, President?"

"No," the other replied, feeling light in the head from his suddenly quickening hunger, "I told you, I don't get angry."

10 Don Roberto

JACINTO'S TRUCK CREPT along the narrow dirt road on the way down to San Martín. Sitting in the front seat, the President caught the first view of town through an opening in the trees to the right. Though it was early, the mist was already gone and the sky and even the white of the buildings in town sparkled.

The town was like food in a huge mouth. The mountains around were the sides of a bowl, and in the middle stood San Martín.

Here was a center of life. The Cabaña of the Indian Institute, the courts, the market, the Cathedral, eighteen churches, ice cream sellers, taxis, the narrow streets and plastered houses with tile roofs. From another opening in the trees the President could see the jail of Santo Domingo, painted pale blue, with its turret where the gunner stood.

Here, after the village, was action and new things to fill the President's mind. Tourists on their way to Guatemala, the smell of frying fish, the blind men who sold lottery tickets. Indians from other villages, and the buses which left for Flores, Oaxaca and Mexico City.

Sometimes San Martín reminded the President of the time before, when he drank.

He left Jacinto's truck at the market, and went inside to

buy meat for his family. Then he led the four Indian policemen with the boy onto a side street going toward Don Roberto's office.

Don Roberto was busy, the secretary said, so the President and his policemen waited in the courtyard.

In his big office, Don Roberto Álba G. sat at his desk holding a report on the living and working conditions for Indian laborers on the coffee plantations in hot country. Don Roberto settled his thin body in his chair and started reading. Then he looked for a cigarette, but could find none in his pockets. A box on the desk held a pack of expensive American filter tips he had filched from his brother's living room the last time he was in Mexico City. He kept them there for show, to offer important visitors. The cigarettes were stale, but Don Roberto lit one anyway.

The lawyer was a second son, and that had made the difference in his life. His older brother was a banker in Mexico City, he owned a pink stucco house on Avenida Aristotle in the plushy Polanco district. When Don Roberto made his yearly trip to the City on Indian business, his brother always took him for an evening on the town to a night club where there was flamenco music and later a show with nearly nude girls. Coming home in his brother's American Buick, Don Roberto would be drunk, and every year he wanted to ask his brother if he had ever read any Aristotle. "You know, the man whose street you live on." Don Roberto had read Aristotle in the University when he was preparing for the law. Sometimes now at night he would read the master again.

In 1930, Don Roberto had learned the law, and came home to San Martín to practice it. He married a pretty girl and had his five children, and when his father died he became master of the huge battered family house which had too many rooms, even for so large a clan. Then, when Cárdenas was still President, they asked Don Roberto to take the job of counsel for the Indian villages around San Martín. Don Roberto was a strange choice for such a job, because he had no special love for the Indians as some of the radical young University men did. But he took the appointment, and as a reward they gave him a seat in the state legislature in Flores.

Until the Indian Institute came to San Martín, Don Roberto worked day and night at his two jobs, neither of which paid him well enough. When the Institute came, and they let him quit the legislature, he had less to do and tried to build a small private practice to sandwich between his various duties for the Indians.

So this morning he had come late to work. He had been out to the village of Santa María to see a client, and had gotten a ride back to town on a friend's truck. He still wore the leather jacket and khaki pants and shirt he had worn out to Santa María.

His secretary, Pepe, a shabby little old man, stuck his head in the door and whispered, "The President is here to see you."

"Which town?" asked Don Roberto, looking up.

"Chomtik."

"Good. What does he want?"

"He didn't say."

"Ask him to come in."

Don Roberto rose to shake hands with the President, intending to make it only a light pass such as the Indians used. But the President of Chomtik surprised Don Roberto, taking his hand firmly like a Mexican.

The two men, about the same age, looked surprisingly

alike. Don Roberto, of course, had lighter skin, and a trim mustache, and the President's hair was thicker, but they both had eagle faces, with high cheeks and sharp, pointed noses. Don Roberto had his unusual blue eyes, and that was a difference also.

"How are things going, President?" asked Don Roberto, smiling.

"Well enough."

"Did you come for something special?" It occurred to Don Roberto that this might be only a friendly visit. The President had his leather bag with him, and it was already full of paper-wrapped packages of meat from the market. Perhaps the President only came to town to buy and chat.

"Yes, I have a boy outside who killed his father."

"Oh, that's a pity."

A pity, the same words the President had used.

The President knew that Don Roberto understood. Not fully, of course, not the way the President understood, not in pictures, but decently, as far as a Ladino could.

"Well," said Don Roberto, touching at all of his pockets for a cigarette, but finding none, "we'll take him over to Santo Domingo in a little while, and arrange the trial then. All right?"

"Yes, that's all right." The President took out his own cigarettes, and gave one to Don Roberto.

"How's your family?" the lawyer asked. "Your boy works at the store there in the village, doesn't he?"

"Yes."

"What's his name?" Don Roberto's high forehead wrinkled, and he stopped to push back his thin hair.

"Eliseo."

"Ah, yes. I shouldn't have forgotten that." Don Roberto smiled.

"Is it funny?"

"The name? No. It was the name of the heaven of the Greeks, wasn't it?"

"I don't know, I saw the name in a book."

"It's also a street in Mexico City, very pretty."

Long ago, when the men from the Institute told him he was going to be taken on a trip to Mexico City, the President had hoped that Don Roberto would be coming also, but the lawyer hated the City, and would not go except when he had to. The President was sorry they had not made the trip together, and sorrier Don Roberto hated the Capital. It would have been a good thing to talk about.

"Would your boy Eliseo like to work in town?" asked Don Roberto, casually, flicking an ash toward the bowl.

"I don't know. I would have to ask him. Would it be work for the Institute?"

The President was suspicious. Not of Don Roberto, because the lawyer had never tried to cheat him. But Don Roberto worked for the government, and the government's method was the favor first, followed by some new duty for the President.

"Why do you ask that?"

There was no need for the President to be guarded now.

"Those of us who go to work for the Institute don't become content," he said. Don Roberto nodded in agreement. "They teach us to want better things, things from town. We learn to live in town, and then the Institute wants us to live in the village."

"But what about yourself? Aren't you content?"

The President smiled. "But I wasn't a young man when the Institute got me. And it's different with teachers. The Institute doesn't teach the teachers to want anything except to make the poor people in the village better."

"Is that what you want?"

"Yes." The President nodded.

The Indian offered another cigarette, which Don Roberto took.

It was pleasant for the President, to sit here and talk this way, while the blue smoke ducked down toward the desk, and then was carried out through the open window. A clock ticked on the wall and there was a picture of López Mateos, the man the President knew, and one of Benito Juárez.

Earlier in the morning, in Jacinto's truck, and then in the market, the President had felt ill. Sick in his stomach and fuzzy in the head, as though he had been drinking. Now he felt better.

"And when your term as President is over, what will you do?" asked Don Roberto. "Be a teacher again?"

"No, I'll go home to the hamlet and plant corn. And when I'm too old and sick to do that, I'll go out in the morning and gather firewood like the children and the old women."

Don Roberto did not quite believe this. He had seen enough of Indian presidents. Life in the village, faster paced, always promising some excitement, became a narcotic for these men. The President was like the others and he would not be able to get away from the village when his term was over.

"A regular Cincinnatus," Don Roberto said, smiling again.

The President looked puzzled.

"Sorry," Don Roberto said. "A famous soldier who lived in another country a long time ago. When the country was in danger he left his fields and went out to battle, and saved the country. Then the people wanted to make him a king, but he went back to his land again."

"That's the better thing to do," the President agreed

when he had heard the explanation. He wanted this kind of talk to go on all morning, but he did not know how to make Don Roberto keep at it.

"What do you want your Eliseo to be? A teacher too? Or President of Chomtik?"

"Someday both," said the President.

"I see. But you don't want him to work for the Institute and to learn to want fine things and to live in town."

"No." The President shook his head. "I want him to have good things." He thought of the fine cut of meat he had right now in his leather bag. Eliseo too had grown used to eating meat. How many other boys in the village could say that? "But I want him to stay in the village."

"Why?"

"He speaks Spanish well. He knows the world. He can help the poor Indians."

The President was showing pride, thought Don Roberto, but only tentative pride.

"What if he came to work for me? My man wants to quit. Your son knows the languages to talk to the people I have to see. I'd pay him well, he could sleep in a room in my house."

The typewriter in the other room had stopped. Old Pepe must be listening. Then it began again, its heavy machine-gun rattle echoing through the office.

"I'll ask him, and if he wants to, he will come to see you."

"Good."

The President waited, thinking that if there there was a string attached, Don Roberto would have to pull it now. The lawyer was always honest with the President and never pretended that a favor and a new duty were not connected.

"President?" asked Don Roberto. "Tell me this: who will they make President after you?"

The other man shrugged. "I don't know."

"Have you thought about it? Isn't it your choice?"

"No—there are other men in the village with more power than mine in these things. Unless I say something, they will pick a certain man named Juan López Oso."

Don Roberto nodded, and placed his fingers together in front of his nose, like a child praying at its first communion. "Ah yes, I know him."

"And one day Jacinto will be President, and perhaps Eliseo after him. I don't know."

"You heard about this Oso and his land?"

The President had not.

"I had dinner at the home of Don Alonso, and he told me he had a new piece of farm land, which he bought from this man in Chomtik named Juan López Oso."

If the President was impressed or interested by this bit of fresh information, he did not show it at once. "Do you like this Don Alonso?" he asked.

The President had been honest with him about the Institute so Don Roberto decided to be honest in return. "One doesn't have to like a man to eat at his table, especially if the man is the richest in the state and the brother of the Governor."

They smiled together.

"I understand," said the President. "But that is Chomtik land—and also, most of it comes from the ejido, and a man cannot sell ejido land."

"That's true," said Don Roberto. "He sold what land actually belonged to him, and the rest—the ejido land—he rented to Don Alonso for ninety-nine years."

"And no one can stop him from this?"

I can't, thought Don Roberto, can you? "I don't know how," he said. "The agreement is secret. Don Alonso only told me about it because he was drunk."

The President cleared his throat, and then remembered he could not spit the phlegm on the floor, and had to swallow it again.

"The Lord gives, and the lords take it away," said Don Roberto, standing.

"What do you say?"

"Nothing." The lawyer smiled. "It's from the Bible. Shall we have a look at your murderer?"

They went out into the courtyard, satisfied with one another, and Don Roberto inspected the boy. Then the two men went out into the crowded streets, to go together to the courtroom at the Cabildo.

The sun was brilliant and made the white walls of the buildings they passed glimmer. There were a lot of Indians in town, hurrying along, followed by their women carrying the loads, like beetles in their black. Chomtikeros standing in doorways raised their hats to the President if they knew him. A pack of Kanalero men sat on a curbstone waiting for the truck back to their village. With their broad-brimmed hats and trailing ribbons of red, blue and purple, they looked like some rare parrots set down among the white Chomtik pigeons.

On a corner of the parque they met Doctor Méndez who told the President he was drunk. The President nodded.

"Let me ask something," said the President when he and Don Roberto stopped under the arcade of the town Cabildo.

"Anything," said the lawyer with a smile. Several attorneys in their blue suits were coming out of the Cabildo and gave him a respectful hello.

The President was having trouble finding his thoughts, and spat twice on the ground. "Do you know the Lacandones, the men who live in the jungle?"

It was a strange question, and Don Roberto took a moment before he answered. "I've read the reports and the books on them—I saw two of their elders once."

"How do they treat strangers?"

"President, why do you want to know?" Don Roberto was disturbed, though less by the questions than by the puzzled look of the President.

"How would they treat a boy who came to live with them, to work in their fields? Would they shoot him with their poison darts? That's all I'm asking."

"They wouldn't kill a stranger—but they don't have much land to till. Mostly they fish. Does the boy you're thinking of know how to fish?"

The President shook his head.

"You couldn't do it *now* anyway," said Don Roberto.

The President looked up from the ground, to his friend. "We could still do it," he said. "We haven't told the judge yet."

Don Roberto didn't like being drawn into the improbable plot, or having to explain to the President.

"It's too late. You have the boy here in town."

"Which would make it easier to get him on a truck, going in the direction of the Lacandones."

"No, my friend." Don Roberto said it as he put his hand on the President's shoulder, feeling desperately the need to touch the man. He understood what the President wanted, and even how the President could think of it. If a man is in the seat of power long enough, he knows how events can be juggled. He sees the wire-pulling go on around him, he feels the yanks on his own cords, and eventually he wants to build a few marionettes of his own.

Don Roberto was convinced now that the President would never leave the village and go back to farming when his term of office was done.

"Let's go inside," he said, and went ahead to lead the way. The President followed.

Don Roberto had thought of explaining the concept of justice, but there was no time, the day was too far gone, and for a moment Don Roberto could not remember how it was he explained justice when called on.

11   Doctor Méndez at the Fountain of Desire

HE SAT WITH HIS HEAVY head in his hands on the steps of the market, thinking how drunk and unhappy he was and how near he had come to getting on Jacinto's truck and safely back to Chomtik. He thought what else was wrong: it was cold on the market steps after sunset, he was almost out of money, he hated his job for the Institute, he wanted to be in Mexico City, he wanted to be a specialist in gynecology, and his mistress had left him for a pharmaceuticals salesman in Flores.

When he felt someone tapping him on the shoulder, he opened his eyes and looked up. Before him stood Mario and the Maestro. Mario's matter-of-fact brown face showed nothing except a little concern, but the Maestro was obviously laughing at him.

"So what is it?" the Doctor asked angrily, thinking for a minute he was in his bed at the infirmary, and they had waked him up in the middle of the night.

"Is there anything wrong?" the Maestro asked him.

The Doctor thought, putting his head back in his hands and rubbing his palms against his eyelids, which created blotchy red circles on the inside. His mind ran over the list of the salient miseries in his life, but he decided not to tell the Maestro. "No," he said. "What are you doing here?"

"Mario came in to buy meat—and I just came for fun," answered the Maestro.

"Left your meat in Chomtik, huh?" The Doctor smiled and tried to stand up. He expected the Maestro would hit him in the face, and he preferred to be standing when that happened.

But the Maestro took the insult.

Maybe, thought the Doctor, he is so stupid he doesn't understand. "Your friend Carla didn't come, huh?"

"That's right," said the Maestro.

"Well, come on." The Doctor nodded. "I'll buy you a drink." He took the Maestro by the arm, for he felt unsteady.

"We were thinking maybe you ought to come back to Chomtik with us now—" the Maestro began.

"With all due haste and great pleasure," Doctor Méndez said. "But there isn't any truck, and I don't feel like walking."

"We'll take a cab then."

"What's the hurry? Let's have that drink." The Doctor began pushing the Maestro down the steps ahead of him.

"We saw the President here, and he doesn't feel well. So maybe we'd better get back."

"Oh, shit!" the Doctor exclaimed. "I saw the President just a while ago and he's fine. Did he go back to the village?"

"With Jacinto."

"Goddamn Jacinto—he saw me running after his goddamn truck but the son of a whore pulled out just as I got to him."

Mario smiled.

They were on the street now, and the Doctor was still tugging at the Maestro's jacket. "Come on," he said. "Don't you worry your cheap little heart—I'll buy everything. I'll even buy for your friend here."

The Maestro looked to be sure the Doctor was joking with Mario, but it did not seem so, until the Doctor put one arm around the Indian's shoulder.

They went with him, hoping that after one or two drinks they could get him to come back to the village. The President had looked pale and barely able to stand up before he left with Jacinto.

The cantina they went to was one small room with red tables and stools, pine needles on the floor and a juke box. The Doctor felt around in his pockets, realized vaguely he did not have much money, and ordered a bottle of cheap clear trago and a large Coca-Cola. The bitter-faced woman who served them filled a bottle from the larger container she kept hidden in the back room and brought it to them.

The Doctor forced them to drink, sloshing trago and then a little Coke into their glasses. Mario drank, but the Doctor had to force the Maestro.

"No, no more for me." The Maestro closed his hand over the top of his glass.

"Well, come on then, this one," the Doctor said, filling

his own glass full. "Half and half." He said salud to the Maestro, tossed off his half, and handed the glass to the other. The Maestro sipped. "Come on—you made the agreement, half and half," the Doctor said.

The Maestro handed the glass to Mario, but Méndez snatched it away and gave it back to the Maestro. "Drink!" He stared hard at the Maestro until he finished the glass.

The Doctor rapped with the empty bottle on the table, and ordered the woman to bring them more.

He turned and clasped Mario on the shoulder. "Mario," he said, closing his embrace on the Indian, "I'll tell you something. Don't ever even think about our women." He paused, looked down and spat on the floor. "You know what I mean?"

"Yes, Doctor, I know."

"Shit if you do! What I'm telling you is our women may look better—they may make you all hot inside—but don't play that way."

"Yes, Doctor."

"And I'll tell you why. You know my woman, my Anna, my darling?"

Mario said, "No, I don't know her."

"Of course you do—you saw her a million times there at the Institute. She worked there, she said she loved me, she made love with me." The Doctor's long bony fingers clutched tightly on the shoulder of Mario's tunic. "And when I came to her last night, they told me at the Institute she has quit her job and gone to Flores to be married. Jesus!"

The Maestro watched Mario. The Indian's square face remained open, showing nothing.

"Well, Jesus—I don't need to tell you this, do I, boy? You don't want our women. You love your own. Right?"

Mario said nothing.

"Here—let's have some cigarettes." The Doctor picked up the soft-drink bottle and rapped on the table. The old woman behind her counter looked up and when she understood what the Doctor wanted, she brought him some cigarettes.

His hands fumbled with the package, and then in anger he ripped the silver paper off the top and poured the cigarettes out on the table. Some rolled away on the floor.

The Doctor looked at them, and then suddenly stood up, knocking over the chair he had been sitting in, and banged away into the back of the cantina to go to the bathroom.

"Don't pay any attention to him," the Maestro said as soon as Méndez was gone.

"I don't."

"We can go to the Institute and see if they will send another doctor."

Mario nodded, and the Maestro wondered where his understanding with this young man had gone. Mario had been quiet since they met the Doctor, and his smiles were hiding something.

"Do you hate him?" the Maestro asked.

Again Mario nodded, quickly as though he had been thinking this at the moment.

It only takes one of us, the Maestro thought.

He saw the Doctor come stumbling back to his chair. Mario picked it up and the Doctor sank into it.

"Here, pour," he ordered Mario, and Mario took the bottle of trago and carefully filled each of the three glasses.

"You know"—the Doctor turned to the Maestro—"I just

talk too much, don't I? I mean why did I even talk that way? They can't love our women anyway. Not real love. Right?"

"I don't know," said the Maestro, self-consciously.

"Come on, then, let's get out of this place." Again, more unsteadily, the Doctor rose to his feet, took his glass and drained it.

The streets were dark and quiet now. The stores which were still open cast bars of pale light across the pavement.

"Come on, let's go!" the Doctor said, stepping into the street, and pulling the others to each side of him with his long arms.

"Where?" asked the Maestro.

"Goddamn it, home! Back to Chomtik."

"You know that's two hours' walking."

"Jesus, of course I know. But what alternative have we got? And your dear friend the President is sick, or something." He stumbled on, pulling the Indian and the schoolteacher with him.

"Here, let's get a little drink," he said when they had crossed the White Bridge and were at the junction where the dirt road to Chomtik, wide and white, veered from the highway.

"Better if we start walking home," said the Maestro. But the Doctor pulled along with his two great arms and the other men were weak after drinking, and cold with the idea of the two hours of walking.

"Just one little beer," the Doctor promised thickly, and led them to a long red and yellow house beside the road. There was a light out front, illuminating the sign painted on the wall—La Fuente de Deseo—but the place seemed closed up. The Doctor rapped on the door, and a window opened. The Doctor explained he only wanted a couple of beers.

"You're drunk," said the voice.

"I am not!"

"Is that an Indian there with you?"

"Yes, but he won't try anything." The Doctor could hear music, the bell sound of a marimba record, and he kicked against the door. A man, shorter than the Doctor, opened for them, and the Doctor pushed inside.

"I'll wait for you," Mario told the Maestro in a low voice. "There, by the corner."

"Come on in," said the Maestro.

Mario shrugged and smiled, and then followed his friend.

The room was bright and clean, with tables and a record player like any cantina. Paper streamers were hung from the strong light in the center of the room. Two doors opened onto a courtyard, and around the courtyard were a number of doors. Two short plump girls sat at a table in a corner, leaning their heads in their hands. They watched the Indian and the schoolteacher and then turned back to the comic books they were reading.

The Doctor got three little bottles of beer and set them down on a table.

"Here, drink up, my friends. Not very alegre here, is it?" He sank onto the bench, not waiting for an answer. The Maestro and Mario crowded onto the seat across from him, with their backs to the two girls.

"Well," said the Doctor, "I talked to the owner, and he'll give us a little credit. I told him I work for the Institute." His black hair had fallen over his forehead, so his wet eyes shone at them as if from the back of a cave. He tilted his head back and drank half his beer.

The music began again, and the Doctor got up and ordered one of the girls to dance with him. She stood up reluctantly.

The Maestro turned around to watch. The Doctor was pressing himself against the girl, but she remained rigid in his arms. When his hand moved down her back she turned herself away from him, as though she was going to leave him.

After the music ended she returned to her table and her comic book, leaving the Doctor standing stupidly in the center of the floor.

"Well, that's all right," he said, smiling as he came back to the table and took his beer. "You look like you were at a funeral. Come on, Maestro, I saved the pretty one for you."

"Let's get going," said the Maestro.

"All right, let's go." The Doctor finished his beer and put it down on the table. He returned to the girls and began dancing with the other one.

She wore high-heeled shoes and a tight blue dress, which showed the round little mound of her stomach. The Doctor pressed against her too, and she responded.

"Half as tall as he is," the Maestro commented to Mario.

When the music ended again the Doctor held this girl and nuzzled into her ear.

She giggled and then let out a little cry. "Don't bite me."

The Doctor laughed. Taking her arm he led the girl to the table.

"This is Dolores," he said, bowing slightly to the two other men.

Dolores giggled again.

"We're going inside there." The Doctor nodded toward the courtyard. His face was red and burning. "Hey, Maestro, she says her friend wants to go along with you. Free, she says. Come on."

"I'll stay here with Mario."

"For Jesus' sake, man, just leave Mario alone! He doesn't want any of this stuff. There's meat for him at home."

The Maestro stood up and walked in front of the Doctor toward the door. "I'm going," he said softly.

"Look, man." The Doctor grabbed his left arm. "Don't worry. They don't love our people, they can't. Just forget it and let's get a little of the stuff. You need it too."

The Maestro could see Mario over the Doctor's shoulder. The assistant was standing up watching them. The Maestro knew the Doctor was drunk and that he himself had been drinking. His ears felt warm. But for a reason he couldn't think of surely, submitting the Indian boy to this was all wrong.

He was shorter than the Doctor, and he was not a fighter. But he spread his legs and swung his free arm wide, so there was a lot of power in his fist when it hit the Doctor, connecting on the left jaw up under the cheekbone.

The Doctor's head turned so suddenly it seemed his neck had snapped. He staggered back twice before he fell, and the girl in the blue dress let out another little cry. The Doctor sat down easily on the floor, almost at Mario's feet.

The Maestro did not look back once he had seen this. He fumbled with the latches of the door, and got outside and started running on the road, not even sure that Mario had followed him until almost half an hour later when the Indian caught up with him in the dark.

12   Mario

IN THE MORNING, MARIO was worried. His father had seemed better on Monday when Mario brought the news that the curer was coming on Wednesday to pulse the old man and find out what his blood said. This morning he sat up on the edge of his bed and drank some corn gruel with warm water. That was good. Then he asked Mario to find him a cigarette, and after searching his own house with no luck, Mario went to a neighbor's to beg some. But when his father had smoked a few puffs, he handed the cigarette back to his son and lay down again on the bed and went to sleep. Mario's mother found some real coffee and made it for her husband very sweet, with plenty of brown sugar. He would not drink it.

Mario touched his father's head and cheeks as he had seen the Doctor do. The old man was very hot.

Toward midday, Mario walked to the Center. He stayed away from the Cabildo as much as possible, and went to the back door of the teachers' house. The girl teacher Carla came to the door and told him the Maestro had gone to San Martín with some people from the Institute. He asked if the Doctor had come back, and she said no.

"How is the President?"

"I don't know. Why?"

"He was sick yesterday afternoon."

"Then why don't you go see him?" the girl said.

Mario nodded and looked away.

Staying out of the plaza, Mario went to the home of his uncle, to find more news. The uncle said the President had returned sick in Jacinto's truck, and was at his home. When the Doctor hadn't come back in the morning, Don Concepción had sent Jacinto on a special trip to San Martín to look for him.

Mario told his uncle why he couldn't go to see the President, and his uncle understood. Then Mario returned home.

He saw his father, ate, and then with nothing to do, he brought a low chair out from his own house, and sat quietly in his yard with his son Pascual. Once he saw Jacinto's merry red truck chugging up the road through the brown valley. Evening came slowly, since clouds still covered the sun. Maruch built up the fire, and asked him if he wanted to come inside. It began to rain, a slight spit of water, and Pascual went inside to sit by the fire. Mario wondered if Jacinto had gotten another doctor from the Institute, and if Doctor Méndez or the Maestro had returned.

Maruch called him again, but he told her he would wait for the older children to come home with the sheep. He was lonely, and could not stand to be with other people.

He began to think the curer would not come, and wondered if he could sneak to the Center the next day, have his wife buy candles, and go pray in the church for his father without being seen.

It was almost dark when he saw the two Ladinos cross over the fence at the bottom of the hill. His children and the sheep were with them. He recognized both men as they came up to him with the children following behind, prodding the sheep.

Both of the men wore Mexican clothes, the taller a blue shirt, the shorter white. The taller man carried a rifle over his shoulder. Mario knew him, he was Miguel López Oso, Juan's brother. They had talked a few times since Miguel had returned to work on Don Alonso's ranch. His head was as narrow as his body, and he had a thin mustache.

The shorter man was named José, and he was also an Indian. Mario had not known that this man too worked for Don Alonso.

They stood beside his fence, as the children ducked through and let the bars down and forced the two sheep over.

"Have you seen rabbits?" Miguel asked Mario in Tzotzil. "We're looking for dinner."

Mario looked away from them. Inside he could hear Maruch stop patting tortillas to listen. He almost wished Miguel had spoken in Spanish, so Maruch wouldn't be able to understand.

"No rabbits around," he said.

"Are those your sheep?" José asked.

"Yes."

"I'm not sure," Miguel said. He ran his fingers through his hair and sighed. "My patrón has sheep like that, and how am I to know your children aren't stealing from my patrón when they come over on my patrón's land with their sheep? How am I to know?"

From the slow way he talked, Mario wondered if Miguel was a little drunk. Or maybe in his years away he had forgotten how to talk. "Those are mine," Mario said. "Also, my sheep were on your brother's land, not Don Alonso's."

He felt himself becoming angry and afraid, and tried to hold in the anger.

"Where's your friend the Paludismo man?" asked José, changing the subject.

Mario was surprised at first that José remembered. "He went away."

José laughed.

Mario tried now for the first time to see their faces, but they stood in the shadow and it was dark.

"Adiós," said Miguel abruptly. José went with him, and Mario could hear their feet going away down the hill in the dark. Finally, when they were at the bottom of the hill, he could see the two figures, until they crossed the fence and were gone.

He went inside to eat his supper. Even the curer will not come tonight, he thought as he ate. Maruch saw he was disturbed, but said nothing until he was finished eating. Then she handed him a banana she had been hiding and saving for the baby.

"Who was the other man?" she asked.

Mario had forgotten she would know the story from the children. "I don't know him," he lied.

Maruch was quiet again.

Mario pressed his tunic down between his knees and put his hands inside across his chest so he could think about this.

It wasn't really his fault that José had gone to jail three years ago. Mario had been carrying out the President's orders. But José would not know or believe this.

It was in the summer before Eliseo's father had become President, when Mario had just started work for the Institute, as a caretaker at the school. One day a bright yellow jeep puttered down the road and into the plaza. On its side was the stark black word PALUDISMO—malaria.

The director from the Indian Institute in San Martín got out with another Mexican and they went to the Cabildo. They talked with the old President, and he called Mario.

It had been reported to the Institute that in some of the hamlets to the north, on the road to San Ramón, the people were sick. Mario knew this was true, he had heard the stories himself. The man from the Paludismo, said the President, was going to the hamlets with medicine and ways to cure people. But he didn't speak Tzotzil, he needed a man to go with him. For five pesos a day would Mario go?

Mario didn't want to, even the money didn't appeal to him, but he actually had no choice—the President had chosen him. So he said he would go with the smiling sallow-faced Paludismo man, and agreed to meet the jeep the next morning at the crossroads above the village.

He waited there in the morning in a heavy rain, and the Paludismo man was late. When Mario got in the jeep the Mexican apologized. Beyond the turnoff to the Center, the road to the north became suddenly steeper, clinging to the sides of hills, descending into one small valley only to begin climbing to another pass. There were stands of big gray wood crosses, and the Paludismo man asked Mario what the crosses meant. Since Mario was away from his home he did not know the names of these crosses. The Paludismo man laughed, and then explained to Mario what he was to say to the people.

They went first to the hamlet of Witzik, where Mario walked from house to house, asking if there were any children sick, or any men and women. He told the frightened people he had come from the President, and the Paludismo man stood at the gate of each house, listening but not understanding. At every house the husband would look suspiciously at the Paludismo man, thinking that some tax would be collected. After a while Mario began to enjoy making his long speech, and explaining that the Paludismo man had good medicine.

When there was a sick child, the Paludismo man would come to the front door and dole out a number of pills, telling Mario how many the child should take every day. The women turned away and hid behind their shawls.

Once, after they had visited the hamlets of Witzik, Cruztik, and were in Koholtik, the Paludismo man found a house where all the people were sick. He said that the house would have to be burned. The man had a shed for corn, and the Paludismo man helped them move a few jars into the shed, and made the women wash the blankets and the clothes. Then they burned the house, because the Paludismo man told them there were bad spirits in it. The flames and smoke were dirty in the hot afternoon sun, and that afternoon Mario was hot and yet proud of his work.

At night Mario and the Paludismo man found houses to sleep in. The Paludismo man had brought along cans of food, some of them with meat, to eat with the women's tortillas. When they could not find a house, they pulled the jeep onto a shoulder of the road, and slept beside it. The Paludismo man would send Mario out to buy tortillas, would build a fire himself, and then read from a book until Mario returned.

They had been gone a week and Mario was enjoying himself. He thought about Maruch and his three children, since he had not told them how soon he would be back. But otherwise the days were pleasant, the food good, and the excitement intense for him when he said he came on the President's business. The Paludismo man was good too, interested in the way the Indians lived, and he began to learn Tzotzil phrases from Mario—"Thank you" and "Your food is good" and "I would like a drink of water."

On the eighth day they moved on to the hamlet of Mutik, where the people were said to be mean. That day nothing seemed strange, except they could not find a house where the men would let them sleep. So they were camped by the jeep in the evening. The Paludismo man was reading his book, and humming to himself. Mario saw a man in Mexican clothes at the top of the hill to the west above the road, and then the man disappeared. A few minutes later Mario heard a soft call, "Brother," which came from the trees behind the Paludismo man's back.

Mario got up, not disturbing the Paludismo man, and walked to the trees. The man would not come out in the open there, but showed Mario where to come into the trees, and led the boy away from the road. When they were well hidden, out of sight of the Paludismo man, the other man spoke in Tzotzil.

"I have something to tell you."

"It's not me you want to see, it's him over there." Mario nodded with his head. In the dark he could barely see the other man's face.

"No, look. I'm an Indian, I'm not one of them. I have my house there in Koholtik."

Mario thought the man was lying, for they had visited all the houses in Koholtik to check for malaria, and he had not seen this man. But from the way he spoke Tzotzil, he probably was telling the truth about being an Indian.

"I was here in Mutik today, on my way home, and the people here are afraid of you."

"Why?"

"Not you. The Paludismo man. They say he is coming to kill them, or take their wives. So they've sent their

women to the hills to stay, and the men in their houses
are all gathered together. They have their guns and are
going to shoot you."

"How did you know this?" asked Mario, trying to get a
look at the man's face. "What is your name?"

"I'm José."

"From Koholtik?"

"Yes, José Pérez."

"Thank you, man." Mario reached out in the dark,
which seemed to startle this José. Then the other man
understood and took the hand Mario offered. In the President's name, Mario thanked him.

"Will you come tell the Paludismo man?" Mario asked.

"No, I have to go home."

Mario returned to the fire, and sat thinking a minute
before he told the Paludismo man.

It wasn't until he began talking that Mario recognized
the loneliness and mingled fears of the thing. He remembered evenings when he was younger, and men would
come together at his father's house, since his father was
an elder of the hamlet. At first only five or six men, claim-
ing that someone was a witch, and they wanted to take
him to the village. Mario's father, speaking from the doorway, would spread his smooth calmness over them, and
they would go away. But later Mario might see them talking among themselves on the road, or at another's house,
and there would be a larger pack of men, some of them
with their hunting guns. Sometime in the night the boy
would hear feet on the road, like horses going by, and then
a single shot, and his father would sigh, as though in his
dream. The next morning the news of the witch's death
would run around the circle of women drawing water, and
Mario would know when he came home from school that

the man was dead. And at the same time, the whole event
would be over. That night no one would hum on the road
and everything would be quiet again. These things were
like a storm. Terrible because no one knew exactly what
would happen when the storm broke. And more terrible
because the land was always the same, unmarked, when
the storm was over.

The Paludismo man's face was calm as Mario told him
about the frightened, armed men in Mutik. The Mexican
said nothing when Mario was through, except that they
would go to sleep now. Mario was in his blanket when he
saw the Paludismo man put his book away in the jeep and
take out a pistol which he put beside him while he slept.

Mario didn't sleep, and early in the morning he thought
of how he would explain to the Mexican without seeming
frightened that he had to go home to see if his wife and
children were well. But the Paludismo man spoke first,
and said they would be going back to the Center for the
day, to get more supplies—food and medicine.

They both left the mountains with relief, though neither
would admit it was more than routine business which
drew them away. When the jeep got back to the village,
the Paludismo man took Mario to the President and Don
Concepción, in the cool of the Cabildo office. While Mario
told his story, in Spanish, the President nodded, and Don
Concepción mumbled to himself.

Then Don Concepción asked for the man's name, and
when Mario gave it, Don Concepción sighed. He looked
at the President, but this President didn't ever talk much,
so Don Concepción went on.

"We know this man, this José Pérez. You're right—he is
an Indian, but he wears Mexican clothes. He has been

terrorizing the poor people in that hamlet off and on for five years."

"Why?" asked the Paludismo man casually.

"We don't know," Don Concepción said confidentially, leaning over to the Paludismo man. "But when a man from Chomtik, an Indian, wants to leave, he wants to burn the place he leaves behind him, or wants to take with him the memory of having been a big man in his home place."

The Paludismo man nodded, and took out cigarettes which he passed to all sitting at Don Concepción's table.

"The Indian, Señor, does not just leave his village all in one day," said the President slowly. "It takes him a long time to tear himself out."

Mario smoked and listened to this talk, feeling very strange. They were talking about Indians, but as though he wasn't one and the President wasn't one. If the Mexicans didn't think of him as an Indian, maybe he wasn't. He remembered his father saying that Mario got work from the Institute because he was an honorable boy. And then his father had told him that more than an honorable boy he would now become a special man. When he heard this from his father, Mario only thought that he was going to be a special man because he spoke Spanish and could write. Now he thought he was special because Mexicans talked this way in front of him. He thought of his wife and wondered if she was special too. Suddenly he was glad he had gone with the Paludismo man, and was willing to go back again, in spite of the danger.

When they returned the next day, Don Concepción and two Indian policemen with rifles came along in the jeep. They drove past Mutik where men were working in the fields and women were sitting on hillsides spinning thread and watching their sheep—nothing strange there. The policemen knew where this José Pérez lived, and left the jeep to go find him.

José came easily, not knowing what was in store. He was small and light and easy-going in the daytime. He was wearing his Indian clothes, and bade the Paludismo man good morning when he came up to the jeep. Then they tied his hands and took him to San Martín, to the bare office of Don Roberto, where Don Concepción dictated a lengthy report about the man.

When he was led away to the court, Mario was waiting in the patio outside Don Roberto's office. The other Indian stopped and looked at Mario and called him cabrón.

Even then Mario knew he had only been doing the right thing. But he was uneasy when Don Concepción told him the next day they were putting José Pérez into the prison of Santo Domingo for two years. Mario had tried not to have any enemies in the world.

When he returned to Mutik with the Paludismo man, the people there, though quiet and suspicious, took the medicine and the Paludismo man had to burn another house. Mario was no longer afraid, and in three more days he returned to San Martín with the Paludismo man. He was given seventy pesos by the Institute, and a gift of cigarettes by the Paludismo man. With the seventy pesos Mario had enough money saved and bought the bit of land by the path from his father's house where he had wanted to build his house.

13 Juan López Oso

THE PANTS WERE A DARK gray cotton, sewn by machine and tapered at the bottom. They were refolded in the package on top of the jacket, and they had become creased. He took them out and hung them on the back of one of his chairs, while his new woman watched.

The jacket was slick leather on the outside, with a zipper and lined with wool. He ran his hand over the wool, and since she smiled at him, he held it out for the woman to touch too. In the bottom of the package was the best—short black leather boots. They were like the ones Don Roberto wore.

After looking, Oso put the clothes away on the shelf in the back of his store, and sat down to listen to his new radio.

Jacinto got lonely when Eliseo had to go away to his father's house, and he could hear the new radio next door, so he went to see Oso.

"Where's your friend?" Oso asked when the younger man was seated by his fire in the back part of the store.

"With his father."

"Is the President going to die?"

"I think so."

Oso sighed. His father and the President had been good friends. He offered to show Jacinto his new clothes. Jacinto was impressed, especially with the black boots.

"When I came back the day before yesterday, I went to buy the things. In the store I met Don Alonso, my brother's patrón: did you know I sold land to him?"

Jacinto said he knew.

"He asked me if I was spending all my new money on the clothes. I told him not all. But I would have spent it all if that was what these clothes cost."

"Then you wouldn't have been able to afford your new woman," said Jacinto with a smirk.

"I didn't have to buy her," Oso said. "She came with me because I told her how I'm leaving here and she wants to leave too."

Jacinto was surprised by this news. "You're going on another trip then?"

"No—I sold my land and I'm going to live in Flores."

"Do you have work there?"

Oso shook his head—no. "But I'll get it," he said.

Once Jacinto had thought of leaving for good himself. But the idea frightened him, and he gave up his plan. Now, hearing Oso's calm assurance, he was frightened for the other man, and excited too.

"Do you know these airplanes?" Oso asked.

Jacinto did, of course. They all had seen airplanes go overhead, and there was a word for them—buzzards with fire inside.

"Do you know what going in one of them is like?" Oso asked, rolling his cigarette between his fingers as though he were gathering excitement from it.

"No."

"Neither does anyone here. Not even the President. But on the street, just on the street in Flores I met a man, just an ordinary man. And he knew. He had been in an airplane and he said to have done that is to know what birds know."

Oso got up, unable to contain his excitement.

"But what about the President?"

"What about him?"

"If he dies they'll make you be President."

Oso could see it—the drunken men after their meeting, with the paper Don Concepción had typed for them, telling him he was the new man. They would be confused when he told them no. He would enjoy their confusion, and the way Don Concepción would wag his old head.

Oso had talked to his brother Miguel about it when he returned from Flores. His brother said that as President Oso could make a lot of money. But then Oso thought of the President still alive: he wasn't a rich man and didn't look as though he would ever be. Miguel said that was only because this President didn't know how to deal with the town people—Don Roberto and Don Alonso and the Director at the Institute. Oso's brother knew, and would help, he said.

"But what do I need that money for?" Oso had asked. "I have enough money from selling my land."

And Miguel had not had a ready answer for that question.

"Do you want to be President, ever?" Oso asked Jacinto. Jacinto had not thought about it.

"To sit there at the Cabildo every day listening to old women and old men from the hamlets crying for your help with their disputes. Huh!" In disgust Oso spat on the floor.

Jacinto agreed. His own life, he felt, was more exciting than the President's. He had the truck and he saw the market and the people in San Martín every day. Even Eliseo, who knew his father well, said there was nothing of interest in the work at the Cabildo. And Eliseo wanted none of it—that was why he had come to work for Jacinto at the store instead of becoming a scribe.

"Have you ever thought of Mexico City? Did you know

there's work for good money to the north in the United States?"

"But the President went to Mexico City," Jacinto objected.

"Because he worked for the Institute—not because he was President," said Oso. "You see?"

Then Eliseo, impassive in the face of his father's crisis and his stepmother's crying, was at the door. He came in, but did not speak. He took the cigarette Oso offered him and smoked in silence.

"I was talking about leaving," Oso said, "and your friend here said they might make me President. What do you think of that?"

Eliseo thought it would happen.

"And your friend Jacinto here said they took your father to Mexico City and I was saying *before* he was President, when he was a Maestro for the Institute in Cruztik. But later your father was President and they didn't care about him any more. He's weak to them, and no use, because he's the President and has to try to stop them, and keep the Mexicans out, so they don't give him any more trips to Mexico City. Isn't that right?"

"Yes," said Eliseo, interested, "because he's President my father is weak."

If Eliseo said it, Jacinto had to agree. They smoked on without talking.

"Look," said Eliseo finally. "My father's woman wants the curer. I was going to get him, but my father wants me to stay. Will you go?"

"Which curer?" Oso asked.

"The one from Lumtik. He was here in the Center yesterday, but now I think he's gone to Mario's house."

"Do *you* want him?" Oso asked.

"I don't know." Eliseo brushed water from under his eyes. He had been crying, but only because the sharp wind outside had blown dust in his eyes. "I don't know, but the woman wants him to come."

"Is your father really bad?"

"Yes."

Oso looked at Jacinto, who was noncommittal, thinking about all the bother of going that far down the road with his truck.

"We'll go now." Oso decided the matter. "On foot."

"Good," said Eliseo. "I've got to get back. My father wants me to read Spanish to him."

"Is he crazy?" Jacinto asked.

"Yes, I think so." Eliseo nodded and then was gone.

14 Mario

IT WAS LATE, TOO LATE for the curer to come, Mario told his mother when she came to his house. They decided at least they themselves could pray. His mother went home and he and Maruch prepared to follow. A heavy misty rain had followed the wind.

Mario was about to go into his father's house when he saw the curer, skittering down the path away from the Center. Mario went inside, stoked up the fire and told his father and mother the man was coming.

The curer was already drunk, and spent a long time warming himself by the smoky fire. Finally he told the sick man to come sit in a chair. Obediently Mario's father got out of bed and sat down.

The women had lost their usual reticence, and watched carefully to see what the curer would do.

The curer took hold of the old man's skinny wrist and held it so he could hear the blood speak. It occurred to Mario that the curer touched his father in the same way the Doctor treated patients, as though they were not people.

There was silence in the house, cut only by the sound of the sticks Mario had put on the fire drying and hissing. For a long time the curer said nothing. Then he dropped the sick man's hand, and called for something to drink.

Mario was too concerned to let one of his younger brothers pour the *posh* for the curer, so he did it himself.

The curer took his drink in a single gulp, and only then did his expression change. He smiled at Mario as though there were some deep secret between them.

"This is good enough. Strong," he said. The curer's face and his hands were wrinkled with age, but his eyes were huge black discs with a special depth to them. Even though the man was drunk and his eyes watery, they betrayed him as a child.

"For my father now?" Mario asked, pouring another glass.

"No. Take that yourself."

Mario, distrustful at this change, drank quickly, and then handed another full glass to his father. He could not remember ever drinking this way, so silent, without toasts.

His father shivered even though he was close to the fire. Mario tried to prompt him, but the patient would not drink immediately.

"Do you know what the blood's saying?" Mario's impatience got the best of him.

For a moment it seemed the curer did not understand,

for he shook his head slowly from side to side. "What? Oh, no, I can't."

"Then you don't know what sickness my father has."

"Some part of his soul is lost."

"What?"

"I'll try again in a minute," said the curer, suddenly sounding tired and not very secret or powerful any more. He leaned forward, took the bottle from Mario and drank from it.

Mario's mother appeared upset by the curer's indecision and strange behavior.

Fortified with liquor the curer took the sick man by the elbow and tried to feel what the blood was saying there in the crook of his arm. The curer leaned close to hear.

"Was this man away in San Martín?" he asked, looking at none of them, staring up into the sooty rafters.

Mario's mother thought. "Yes," she said, "a month ago."

Well, the curer thought part of the soul might have been lost in San Martín, but he didn't know what part yet.

"Do you have a chicken ready?"

Mario was relieved. If the man was asking for a chicken it meant he would soon be holding the ceremony for the return of the soul.

"Yes, I have a good chicken outside. Do you want to kill it tonight?"

"Well," said the curer slowly, his large eyes still fixed on the ceiling beams, "bring it, we'll see."

Mario went outside in the dark. He didn't see the two men hurrying down through the pass from the cross of San Pedro until he had gotten the chicken, a fat one, by the legs, and was returning to the house. They came up on him fast, and were panting by the time they got to his doorway.

"Mario?"

"Who's there?"

"Oso and Jacinto."

"Good. You've come. Get inside here." He wondered what they would want.

Mario threw open the door for them and led the way inside, the chicken still flapping in his hand.

The two men were glad to see the curer. Jacinto's face rounded with pleasure. "My uncle," he said, "is very bad, so you are to come right now."

The curer was unimpressed. "There are plenty more curers, go get one of them."

Oso wiped his wet hair from his face. "But you are the best, Uncle, and the President must have you tonight." Oso's voice was stern, and the curer stood up.

Mario dropped the chicken, and after a squawk it hobbled away unnoticed toward the dark corner by the bed. Mario knew he had better not say anything, but his anger hit him suddenly like cold wind.

"Well then, let's go," said the curer, smiling the secret smile. He was drunk and resigned to a never-ending series of sicknesses which had carried him from hamlet to hamlet like a blown leaf or a black bird for over a week now. He gave in to Oso's command because a command is easier to follow than the plans one's own mind can make up. The curer hoped, secretly, that in some house he visited they would forget about him for a while, and he would be able to curl up by the fire and sleep.

"My father is sick too," Mario said softly.

"Are you ready?" Oso asked, stepping toward the door. He pretended not to have heard Mario's protest.

The curer took up his leather bag. He found his hat by

the bed, and put it on over his bandanna. Then he noticed the chicken.

"Here—you!" He pointed a shaking finger at Mario. "You come. Bring that chicken with you."

"My father," whined Mario.

"We'll come back when we've seen the President, boy. Come on!"

Mario expected his own father to say something. But the shivering old man was still sitting in his little chair, staring into the glass of trago his son had given him.

On the rutted steep paths, Oso and Jacinto went first. Mario followed with the curer, who walked as though in his sleep, stumbling as he went. The chicken trembled and fluttered from time to time, banging against Mario's cold leg. He had not had time even to fold back the chicken's wings.

Tomorrow he would take his father to the clinic at the Institute in San Martín, he thought. Maybe no one would recognize him, or maybe they would forgive him.

The village was almost invisible in the dark as they came down into the valley. A light was on in Don Concepción's house as they came by the Cabildo. But the infirmary was dark: maybe the Doctor still hadn't come back.

So, hoping for this and with a chicken flapping against his leg, Mario went along with the others to attend the President's death.

15   The President

HE HAD FELT SICK FIRST
when he left Don Roberto after talking to the judge at the
court. It was late when he went back to the market to look
for Jacinto's red truck. Jacinto was waiting for him, and
they left for Chomtik, the President riding in the cab. At
first, while they were leaving town and still picking up
passengers, the President hugged his own chest inside his
tunic.

"Uncle, do you mind if we stop a while? I want to get a
drink." Jacinto had parked the truck before a one-room
store on the edge of town.

"Will you go on, Jacinto. I'm sick."

Jacinto asked where, and the President said in the heart
and in the stomach.

"Well, Uncle, then I'll take you back to the Institute to
see one of their doctors. Wouldn't that be better?"

Jacinto's voice was solicitous, but the President felt
again that this was the boy's false politeness. He asked
Jacinto just to get to the Center as quickly as possible.
They passed on up the road, through Lumtik, where the
President could see a few school children playing basketball on the court perched above a deep ravine, and where
he could pick out his own house, shuttered now and
locked, with the grass growing around it. They got beyond
the place where Don Alonso had his ranch, with the fruit
trees, and the big white house set back from the road. The
truck lurched around each turn as Jacinto went faster than

usual, and faster than it was safe to go on the narrow road. When they got to the village the President had to ask Jacinto to help him to his house behind the infirmary.

He went to bed and waited. In the evening he would not eat. He was waiting for Eliseo to come, and it was late before the boy arrived accompanied by Jacinto. Eliseo asked how his father was, and then they fell back into silence. Uncomfortable, the boy turned on the radio.

"Please come here, Eliseo," the President said when he could stand the radio no longer. He reached for a chair and placed it beside the bed for the boy to sit on. Eliseo came, unwilling but obedient.

"Do you remember the year you lived in Cruztik with me at the school?"

The boy nodded.

His father had wanted to say something about Eliseo's mother. But the other woman was here now, surrounded by her own children, and with his new baby son, so he did not talk of his real wife.

"Do you remember what they do there with the dogs when the corn is ripe and almost ready to be picked?"

"Yes," said Eliseo, speaking in Spanish. "They tie the dogs' legs in front so they won't jump up and get at the corn. Why, Father?" Eliseo was reciting, from time to time stealing looks at his friend Jacinto, whom the President couldn't see from the bed.

"I wanted to know if you remembered that. I've never seen the men do that in any of the other hamlets."

"But they do," Eliseo insisted, turning in his chair, staring away from his father.

"Where, boy? Which hamlets?"

"I don't know, Father." The boy got up and borrowed a

cigarette from Jacinto, then sat down again. Seeing this, his father took his own pack out of his shirt pocket, and gave it to the boy.

"Don't you want these any more?"

"No."

"All right." Eliseo put the cigarettes in his own pocket.

It occurred to the President that since they were talking Spanish, he could safely ask the son what he remembered about his real mother. Instead, he continued to worry about the dogs in Cruztik.

"Do you know which hamlets, boy?"

"In all of them, Father, if you look carefully enough. They tie up all the dogs in one way or another."

"But they all don't hobble the dogs, as they do in Cruztik."

"Remember, Father? In Cruztik the men sit outside with their shotguns in September, and shoot the dogs if they get loose in the corn."

"That's right," the President said, thinking back.

He wanted the boy to go on talking. Hearing Eliseo talk was like reading a picture book. You never knew what would come next, what pleasures there would be to fill you next.

"Do you remember my telling you about the dogs I saw in Mexico City?"

"The ones of the rich people there. And the men from the Institute told you those dogs eat meat every day—sometimes twice in a day."

"Yes." That was the memory the President wanted to hear repeated to him. "Do you believe it?"

"No," said Eliseo, drawing on his cigarette.

The pain and nausea had been constant since he got

into the truck with Jacinto in the afternoon. It was less when someone was talking to him.

The next morning old Don Concepción offered to go into town to look for the Doctor. And he promised that if he could not find Méndez he would bring another one from the Institute. But the President did not want this. He did not really want to see the Doctor, he said. He would be better in a day or two.

His woman was worried when he wouldn't eat, and went to the stores in the village to buy him the things he liked especially—sardines, and a tin of sweet crackers. He wondered all day why Eliseo didn't come, and once when the woman was out he got up and threw his tunic over his head, without buckling it, and went to the doorway. From there he could see the line of stores. Eliseo was sitting on the front stoop of Jacinto's, strumming the Mexican guitar he had bought. The record player of the store was on, and Eliseo was playing one of the songs he liked best. The words came clearer than usual. The President started to call out to his son, but went back to bed.

Toward nightfall he was too tired to fight the woman any longer; she talked constantly of sending for a special curer she knew from Lumtik. The President did not want the curer, just as he did not want the almost constant line of scribes and officials who came to stand outside the house and beg to come in and talk with him. None of them had anything to say once he had shaken hands with them or touched their bowed heads.

He agreed that the curer could be sent for, but asked that Eliseo not go. Instead Eliseo was sent to get one of his schoolbooks and read Spanish to his father. He let the boy pick any one of the familiar lessons, and so he heard again the story of Benito Juárez's terrible childhood. How he was an orphan, and half an Indian, but he went to school to study to be a priest, but instead he had become the savior of Mexico and the Giver of the Reforms.

Juárez, in the pictures, had a round face, more like Jacinto's than Eliseo's, but from his days as Maestro the President remembered how he had thought of the similarities between his own son and the great President of the Republic. Both orphans, both students, both Indians, both with the same liquid and intent eyes. Maybe, the President thought, it was because of himself that Eliseo would not become a great man. Maybe you have to be a real orphan, instead of a half orphan. Or maybe you can only be half Indian.

Or maybe it never happened with Juárez the way the children's reader said. The people at the Institute always wrote to encourage the schoolboys to learn, and to study their reading. Maybe the Juárez story could only happen once, as the priest in San Martín had told the President the Christ story could only happen once.

They brought the curer, and there was a chicken fluttering around the house, upsetting the fire. The President would not get up and sit in a chair to have his pulse heard, so the curer, who was drunk, had to sit in Eliseo's seat, while the boy stood impassive behind him, still holding the school reader in his hands. The curer tried to make the President take a drink, and his woman encouraged him, and Oso, and Jacinto. He wanted to tell them what drinking had done to him once, but it was too long a story, and it was about his real wife.

He remembered that coming through the market the afternoon before he had seen the Second Alcalde waiting at the gates of Santo Domingo for the boy who murdered his father. The President had been lax, he should have told the little craftsman not to go to town for several days, since the boy would be having his trial, and the Second Alcalde could teach him nothing about making bags in that time. He told Oso about this and gave him ten pesos more to hand over to the Second Alcalde.

It hurt him to cough and clear his throat, and he didn't like to lift his head since it made him dizzier, so he merely turned to the assembled crowd and spat toward the floor. Even this was uncomfortable, and he wondered if the sickness was in his heart or his head or where he breathed.

He died when it seemed he was asleep, though no one could tell any more, not even the curer, since they were all drunk and sitting by the fire.

PART **TWO**:

JUAN LÓPEZ OSO

16 Juan López Oso

THE OFFICIALS DID NOT
know what to do when the old President died. Many of
them journeyed to Lumtik for the funeral and got drunk.
But two of the Gobernadors stayed behind to talk with
Don Concepción. They were uneasy since they did not
speak good Spanish, and did not know if talking about a
new President was their duty or not.

Don Concepción switched to Tzotzil, gave them cigarettes, and told them they must have a meeting, which was called for the next day.

Some of the officials were still drunk or sleepy, and dozed off on their chairs in the Cabildo. Others wore their black wool tunics and their ribboned hats and held their canes of office. But the meeting was in fact less than a ceremony. Don Concepción told them they should do what they wanted about a new President, and before he was through talking a mumbled consensus had been reached, and the oldest of the Alcaldes announced they would go right away to Oso's house.

So the forty men trooped across the plaza, and found Oso waiting in his doorway. There was a grin on his face when they told him what they wanted, and he said he would think about it and tell them at the Cabildo the next morning.

Late in the afternoon, Oso walked down to Lumtik to talk to his brother Miguel at Don Alonso's ranch. The hacienda was a long white-plastered building with a porch, deep inside the grounds of the ranch, and surrounded by fruit trees. Everything was very still. Oso found his brother sitting in the shade on a stool, with a saddle across his lap. Miguel was replacing the worn-out leather thongs which held on the stirrups, and it seemed to Juan his brother was the king here.

"Ho, Juan, what's new?" His brother spoke in Spanish.

"Nothing. The President died."

"I heard that. Here, sit down." Miguel pointed to another stool near him which Juan dragged closer. The older brother called for one of the girl servants, who brought a bottle of trago from inside the house.

"You drink Comiteco now?" asked Juan, looking at the bottle on the ground.

"That's right." Miguel poured two glasses, picked one up and drank it. "Costs more, but it's better than Indian stuff."

Juan picked up the bottle and held it. "How much?"

"That was twelve pesos a liter."

Juan nodded. He drank his own drink, and wondered how rich Miguel was by now. "They want to make me President out there," he said slowly.

"Who does?"

"The officials."

"What about the Institute, what about that lawyer in San Martín?"

"They won't object."

Miguel went back to his work, taking one of the thongs in his teeth while he tied it to the saddle. "Do it," he said finally.

"Why?"

"You want to make money, don't you? Those people are sheep to be sheared, Juan."

"But I was thinking of going away."

"Where?"

"Flores, maybe Mexico City."

His brother had nothing to say for a moment.

It occurred to Juan that he was planning to do what his brother had done many years ago. And now Miguel was back. Juan didn't know why, but he sensed his brother had failed in some way. He wanted to know why, but didn't feel he could ask Miguel.

"Have you ever been in an airplane, Miguel?"

Miguel shook his head—no.

"That's one thing I want to do."

"But think of the money you can make here as President."

"I don't need more money."

Miguel dropped the thong from between his teeth and laughed. "You haven't thought about it, Juan. Or you still think of money like an Indian does. Look, I can help you, show you how—what do you think you can make as President out there in a month?"

Oso picked at the hairs on his chin and then said, "Three or four hundred pesos."

"Eight hundred, a thousand I say."

"No." Oso laughed. His brother had been reckoning money too much as Mexicans did. He had forgotten what Indians had.

It was very still around them, and secret. "Look," Miguel said, "think of it this way. Every day the President of Chomtik listens to how many cases? Three? Four? That's a lot of work for him, a lot of talking. And what does he get for it? Maybe sometimes they bring him a bottle of *posh*, which he has to share with the officials. Two pesos' worth of trago, and the old fools from the hamlets, what have they done to deserve part of that reward? Nothing. You know that. But what if the President charged each side in a case something small—two or three pesos— six pesos in all? Not a lot of money, six pesos. But the President puts it in his pocket, and in a month he has nearly five hundred pesos or more just from cases. You see?"

"Yes, I see."

"Or what about this, Juan? Men come to the President to get a release from the national conscription so they can go away to work on the plantations in hot country, and make a lot of money. What if the President charges each of these men five pesos for their papers? You see?"

"Yes."

"If you listen to me, Juan—"

"I see." He knew his older brother was right, but he was not sure about anything. "I will think it over."

"Here, have another drink," said Miguel. They drank again and Miguel went on working. Finally Juan said he had to go and walked back to the village in the twilight.

When he got there his woman said the Maestro had come several times to see him. He thought of going to the school, but decided to wait.

The Maestro came again after dark, and invited him to come for a drink. As they were crossing the plaza the Maestro told Oso how sorry he was about the old President.

"And you know—" he said finally, "well, you heard about my fight with the Doctor. I've been thinking about it all day. The Doctor was drunk, and probably couldn't have done anything for the man anyway."

Oso agreed.

"But still, I feel badly about it. For if the Doctor had been here—and it's my fault that he wasn't—"

Oso laughed at this. "You gave the Doctor what he was looking for."

The Maestro laughed too.

They went into the kitchen at the teachers' house, and sat down. The Maestro brought a bottle of brandy from his room and pointedly told his woman Carla to go away. She went and the Maestro stood up, raised his glass and said softly, "To the new President of Chomtik."

Oso laughed and drank before saying he might not take the office.

The Maestro's square, boyish face showed astonishment in the kerosene light. He put his hand on Oso's shoulder and looked at him closely.

"Why, man?"

"I want to live away, to work in Flores."

"But man—" The Maestro sat down again. "I'm very surprised at this. In fact, I was just waiting for the time you would become President. Not that I didn't like the man who died. In effect, we at the Institute had a lot of respect for him—after all, he was one of us, of the Institute himself, wasn't he?"

Oso nodded, but thought to himself, No, the old man was an Indian.

"But anyway, I was hoping for you. The old man was just, and smart, you know he was smart—but he was old. He thought in the old ways." The Maestro smiled self-consciously. "Not that those ways aren't good enough. But as you know, we at the Institute, well, we look for the civilization of the Indian. Not only do we want progress, we want this to be the best Indian community in the state of Chiapas, in all of Mexico for that matter. You understand what I mean?"

Oso said that he did.

"Here, let me give you an example. Out in the hamlet of Pahalum the Institute built a mill to grind corn—remember that? So the women wouldn't have to spend all day working at those inefficient metates. A good idea. A lot of the Institute's money spent. The men out there supported the idea, in fact, they built the house for the mill. We taught a man how to run the mill, and the Director himself came out from San Martín to open it. Everything ran well."

The Maestro poured another set of drinks, drained his and went on. "Until—until the men found out their women were using the time while they waited for the corn to be ground to talk, to gossip. So the men got together and came to the old President. Remember that? And they said they didn't want the mill. They said it made their women lazy, turned them into bad wives. And the old President let the men close down the mill, and the women went back to their slavery at the metates. Would a strong man do that, let the men from Pahalum have their way like that?"

"Because a man is President," said Oso slowly, "it doesn't mean he is strong enough to tell everybody in all the hamlets what they can do."

"I know that, man, but remember, I'm talking about you, not about the old President. Look at you, you're strong in your body, and in your mind. The old man wasn't. He didn't know what he wanted, and you do. That itself will make you strong."

Oso shrugged, pleased with the idea that he was better than the old President.

"Let me tell you something," said the Maestro earnestly. "This will be hard to understand. Do you know why the Institute is here in this village, teaching the children, helping the sick, building roads, helping pay for Jacinto's truck, doing all those things?"

"To help the poor Indians," said Oso.

"Yes, of course. But do you know why? Here, let me explain." The Maestro sucked in on his cheeks, and then began. "Mexico is a big country, very big. Every day Mexico is learning more, the country is getting richer and has more power. There are millions of people working for this goal. Do you understand?"

"Yes."

"But there are also the Indians. The Indians work for themselves, not for all of Mexico. They don't want to learn to make more, to produce more. They say they are happy enough when their children are fed. But look at it this way, Juan. In San Martín there are almost as many people as there are in Chomtik. But the people in San Martín work in town, they don't have the land to grow corn to make their tortillas. So some Mexican has to grow enough corn to feed his own family and the family of a man in town. You understand? But the Indian doesn't think of this. The Institute wants to teach him to grow more corn— but will he learn? No. He says he has enough for himself. Maybe he does, but he sees no farther than his own little hamlet. He doesn't see the great goals of all Mexico."

Oso thought a moment, while the Maestro poured another shot of brandy. Oso did not see why he should be growing food for the Ladinos in town. They had more than he did to begin with. Why didn't Don Alonso do that work?

But something the Maestro had said hit him, and so he said quietly, "That's what I want, to see Mexico. The Capital, all of it, the airplanes."

The Maestro understood. "Well," he said, gravely, "I can't promise you—but the Institute might take you to Mexico City, sometime, if you are President. To see what we mean about how the Indian must think of the whole country, not just himself."

The Maestro looked up into Oso's eyes, to see if his bribe had had its effect. For a moment Oso's eyes stayed dead, then his gold teeth showed in his big face, and the eyes seemed to catch fire.

"Good," he said, standing up.

"You'll be President then!" the Maestro exclaimed, clapping Oso on the shoulder, and in his enthusiasm pumped the other man's hand.

"I don't know yet. I'll have to think about it."

The Maestro knew enough to understand what this

hesitation meant. These Indians seemed to be the masters of their own fate. Their wives were like possessions, following behind meekly on the paths, carrying the burdens. But an Indian never made a big decision in one day, he always said he would think about it. Which meant he would talk to his wife. Men are the same the world over, thought the Maestro, as he happily went about his business knowing that he himself had persuaded Oso to take the job.

Oso told no one directly that he would be the new President. But on Friday he came to the Cabildo where a number of the officials were sitting on the wooden benches, morose, sleeping in the sunlight, or playing with the fringes of their tunics, and he told all present they must bring fireworks, skyrockets, when he received the cane of office on Sunday.

Then Oso's face showed surprise—raised eyebrows and half smile, like a man getting angry.

"And I don't have a black tunic to wear. I must have one of those." Having given his orders he stalked away across the plaza, leaving the old officials to provide as well as they could. One of the scribes said he would go to town to buy the fireworks if they gave him money, and a decrepit Gobernador thought of going to Lumtik to see if Eliseo would sell his father's black tunic.

In Lumtik the Gobernador found the old President's house, and came upon the wife, still drunk from the funeral. She said Eliseo was not there, she had not seen him. Before she would speak she tried to force herself to vomit by putting her finger down her throat.

The Gobernador found Eliseo not far away from the house, crumpled in the weeds behind a sheep pen, drunk but not asleep, singing a Mexican song to himself and the sky. He was abashed about being drunk, but still drunk enough to be happy. The Gobernador tried to get Eliseo to stand up and walk, but only brought the boy to a sitting position.

"A man shouldn't drink—he must not!" said Eliseo vehemently. "My father drank too much, when he was a Maestro. But he stopped. My godfather would not stop—drinking every day—and he died."

"Eliseo? I came to ask about your father's black tunic."

"But what does a man do when he's sad? What else is there to do?"

"I came to ask for the black tunic your father wore as President—I want to buy it," said the old official.

"Oh," Eliseo said, looking up, seeming to comprehend. "Yes. My father had a black tunic. You know why? Because his heart was sad. You know why?"

"No." The Gobernador was patient.

"Because he wouldn't drink and be happy—that's why he was sad." Eliseo fell down again, and stared up at the sky. The weeds made a half-roof over his head, and he felt hidden and alone. The damp smell of sheep dung seemed to be in his clothes and he wondered how it had gotten there.

Later when Eliseo was able to go home, the Gobernador talked the matter over with the wife as Eliseo sat dumb and nodding. They agreed on eighty pesos for the black tunic. A low price, and they all knew it, but what else could you do, thought Eliseo, when a man comes to you to buy something when you are still drunk.

The next day Eliseo came back to the village, sober, and got the tunic from his father's house to take to Oso. He could not understand why Oso himself had not come to him and asked for the tunic. Eliseo would have given it as a gift, and as thanks in the name of his father for Oso's taking the job.

His father wanted Oso to be President, thought Eliseo. He had almost said so when he gave Oso the ten pesos to deliver to the Second Alcalde.

Eliseo would not have worn the tunic himself, though it was still new, the wool thick and matted and glistening with almost-hidden oily colors in the black. It would be warm for Eliseo, but too big—Jacinto would laugh at him if he wore it.

"President? I've come," he said at the doorway of Oso's store.

Oso's new woman came to open the door. Oso himself sat in a little chair and lightly shook Eliseo's hand when he came in.

"Here's the tunic."

"Good. Put it down."

Eliseo left the tunic on the table. He started to sit down himself, but he remained standing.

"Did they pay you for it?"

Eliseo said yes, and gave the price. Oso grinned.

"You've decided to do it then?" asked Eliseo.

"Yes."

"Why?"

Oso looked to his woman, but she didn't have the answer either. "I don't know," he said.

"Well, it's good."

Oso remained still.

"Are you sad about something?" Eliseo asked.

"Yes, for your father."

Eliseo nodded, but did not believe this. At first he thought Oso had that vague quiet of a man who is getting over being drunk. Then it seemed something more, as though Oso were older all of a sudden. Eliseo wondered if just becoming President changed a man like this. If it were true, he had lost another friend the same way he had lost his father.

"In the morning," said Oso, "in the middle of the market, at nine, I want you to get the loud-speaker ready, so someone can talk through it, saying that I will be the new President."

"Who's going to talk? You?"

"No. The Maestro, or Don Concepción. One of the Ladinos. To tell everyone there they must come to the courtyard of the church to watch."

"I see, President," Eliseo said.

When his own father had received the cane of office, it had been different. The first day of the new year, no announcements on the loud-speaker from the record player. Eliseo's father had been humbled by the occasion, nervous, unsure he was doing the right thing.

"Do me this favor," said Oso. "Go now, over to the Cabildo, and tell whatever officials are there that tomorrow I want them to wear their hats with the ribbons, their black tunics, and their necklaces. And the ones who have canes, the Gobernadors and the Alcaldes, they are to bring them. And the wives of the officials too—with their necklaces."

"Yes, President."

The idea of the ceremony seemed to grow in Oso as he talked about it. "And trees. Tell them I want pine boughs set up as trees in the path from the gate to the church, the way they do for Carnaval and the fiesta of the Patrón."

"Like for the procession of the saints?"

"Yes."

Eliseo knew all of these preparations, especially finding

the pine, would take the officials the rest of the afternoon. So before Oso could issue more orders, the boy excused himself and ran off to the Cabildo.

Because there was no court, and because it was Saturday, the village had been dead or sleeping that afternoon. The few Mexican women from town who set up stands to sell coffee and bread on market day were there, already tending their charcoal fires, making places under vacant store fronts for their myriad children to sleep overnight. Otherwise the plaza had been quiet—as though people were saving their energies for the market next day.

But suddenly it was more like the day before Carnaval begins, or the fiesta of San Juan. The officials, worried, set off for the surrounding hills to bring in the pine boughs. Someone said if there were to be trees in the courtyard, there should also be pine needles spread on the floor of the church, as for any fiesta. So others set out to gather pine needles. The scribes joined together in the Cabildo waiting for the older men to come back so they could do the work of setting up the trees. The few officials with nothing to do could not stand the excitement, and went home to brush their black tunics for a fiesta.

The next morning was cold, with a misty rain; by six o'clock women from the hamlets were seated on the ground in the best spots before Jacinto's store, arranging little pyramids of fruit on their shawls. By seven, men coming into the valley with mules laden with sacks of corn were pushing themselves and their animals into a trot the last part of the way to get the remaining decent places in the market. Before eight two trucks arrived with Mexican men who would sell tin griddles and the larger, factory-made clay pots. The rain stopped and a weak sun started burning its way through the clouds. Eliseo was up, and on

Jacinto's order played some Mexican songs over the loud-speaker at the store.

Those officials who had them were wearing their broad-brimmed hats trailing red and green ribbons, and their women followed behind with necklaces and their best black shawls over their heads. Many of the officials with-out canes or staves carried sticks of fireworks over their shoulders, and in the courtyard of the church someone lit and let go a few skyrockets.

No one in the market had seen Oso. His store was locked, and not even his woman was there. Eliseo won-dered what he should do, since it was now after nine. Per-haps, he thought, Oso left last night for Flores, to ride in airplanes.

But Oso had been waiting in the Cabildo. Now he came across the plaza flanked by two shorter figures—the Mae-stro and Don Concepción. Seeing them coming, Eliseo plugged the record player and loud-speaker into the bat-tery and waited. The officials, coming from all parts of the market, gathered around the porch of Jacinto's store.

Eliseo gave the microphone to the Maestro, who blew into it several times, and then started speaking in Spanish.

Oso was wearing the black tunic, and had on his new boots. Don Concepción held the cane in his hands.

"The President of this village of Chomtik, Antonio Hernandez Pérez, has died. The officials of the regional and constitutional assemblies of Chomtik have met, and there is a new President, Juan López Oso, of the barrio of San Pedro—"

Oso interrupted him and told Eliseo to turn up the loud-speaker. Not everyone in the market had stopped to hear the Spanish they could not understand, so Oso had the Maestro start again. When he was finished, Don Concepción took the microphone and repeated the same message in his gravelly Tzotzil. The officials nodded when Don Concepción ended with the instruction that everyone was to proceed to the courtyard of the church and they began to move off toward the church, pulling a large part of the crowd with them.

Oso waited until many of them had gone, then told Eliseo to come with him, and walked to the churchyard. The trees had been set up as he ordered on the path to the big cross in the center of the yard, and as he entered the gate the scribes began setting off skyrockets with cigarette butts, and the sacristan atop the face of the church caught the signal to begin striking the biggest of the three bells. When Oso, flanked by the Maestro and Don Concepción and followed by the bewildered Eliseo, reached the cross and turned, the officials and their wives kneeled. The people from the market, many of them, kneeled too. They were astonished, not having expected such a great show.

"What I'll do now is give this thing to you," said Don Concepción to Oso confidentially.

"No, give it to the boy there." Oso pointed to Eliseo.

Don Concepción gave the cane to Eliseo, and Eliseo held it lightly, as though it were hot.

Suddenly Oso kneeled, quickly, with no confusion, as if he had been shot in the stomach. Then he looked up, cradled the silver tip of the cane in his big hands, and kissed it once.

"I accept the post of President of the constitutional and regional assembly of this village, Chomtik," he shouted. "For the sake of the Patrón San Juan." There was no hesitation in his voice, and the sound echoed in the stillness of the walls of the church.

He stood, took the cane under his right arm, and faced

the scribes waiting by the arch of the church's yellow and blue front portal. They did not know what he wanted, then suddenly understood and puffed on their cigarettes to get the hot coal to light more fireworks. As the sky-rockets gushed sparks and shot off, and the bell began its uneven clang again, Oso strode to the church, leaving the Maestro and Don Concepción and Eliseo behind.

Once inside he could smell the fresh pine needles. He was pleased the officials had remembered this, though he himself had forgotten. Self-confident, he strode to the altar, the new cane under his arm. There he waited. But he didn't turn. He stayed ready, hearing the sounds of padding feet, and the soft voices of many people crowding into the church, and he began to pray to the image over the altar, calling aloud.

"San Juan, Patrón. I take the cane of the President in your name. I seize it here at the black tassel, and will protect it and your place, Chomtik, with my heart and my life."

The officials listened carefully. They were used to mumbled prayers to the Saint, a kind of holy confusion in any man who approached the altar where the Patrón stood. Several of the older men cried.

To everyone it was a fiesta they had not expected. Somehow Oso had made it a great day. The Maestro was proud. Don Concepción could see what the new President was doing with these Indians, and Eliseo wondered why he had been called on to present the cane to Oso, this new Oso.

They were impressed, even after Oso disappeared in the afternoon. Even with him gone it remained a fiesta day, the officials got drunk together, and many of the people who had come simply to the market remained late in the day, drinking and talking. They stayed until nearly dark, and didn't get home until the paths were too black to see.

17 Eliseo

THE DOCTOR RETURNED on Thursday, riding with Jacinto in the cab of the truck. There was a clean white bandage on his left cheek and he seemed leaner and more cold than ever. He took his things from the front seat and turned to Eliseo.

"I was sorry to hear about your father."

Eliseo shrugged. There was no feeling in the Doctor's voice.

"But I had this problem." The Doctor touched his cheek lightly.

"Does it hurt you still?" Eliseo ventured.

"I lost teeth."

Eliseo nodded.

"Have you seen Mario?" asked Méndez.

"He's there at the infirmary. He's been waiting for you."

"Good. I want to talk to him."

"Will you talk to the Maestro?"

"After I've seen the new President."

A few minutes later, when the Doctor had gone to the infirmary and shut the door after him, Eliseo closed the store and went to the Cabildo. The officials were sitting listless in the sun outside, but the new President was working inside with Don Concepción. The Secretary was typing a list.

Oso looked up and smiled when Eliseo came in. "So the Doctor came back. What does he have to say?"

"Nothing," answered Eliseo. "He's coming to see you."

"Good," said Oso. "Maybe you should go to the school and tell the Maestro to run away and hide." Then he laughed, and Eliseo laughed with him.

"Come take a look at this." Oso beckoned, and Eliseo went to peek over Don Concepción's shoulder. The old man was typing a list of men from the hamlet of Nichimal released from national conscription. "All of those going to finca?" asked Eliseo.

"Yes," said the Secretary.

The boy was unimpressed, he had seen his father writing these lists many times. He turned to Oso.

"The difference is that this time it costs fifteen pesos a man." Oso smiled.

"It used to be two," said Eliseo.

"In the old days." Oso smiled again.

A man Eliseo recognized vaguely called from the doorway, "President, President?"

Oso walked out to him and took his hand, and Eliseo followed. "You've come, Brother-in-law," Oso said, but if he was glad to see the man Salvador he did not show it.

"My son said you had become President."

"That's right."

"I have to talk with you."

"Well, what is it?" Oso asked.

Eliseo was sure Oso already knew the request.

"Now you're President, aren't you? And I don't have to be Gobernador from my place this year." Salvador smiled happily.

The Doctor was walking slowly across the plaza toward the Cabildo, wearing a clean white shirt and black trousers. He seemed in no hurry to come and stopped midway to look around him, brush his long hair from his eyes, and light a cigarette.

Eliseo thought that if he ever became a Ladino himself, it would only be when he could have the bearing and assurance of the Doctor. None of these ragged Indians in Mexican clothes who lived on the road to San Martín and were more miserable than Chomtikeros themselves.

When the Doctor came on the porch, Oso turned to him, seeming to forget the man Salvador.

"President," the Indian whined.

"I have a lot of business today, come back tomorrow." He smiled at the Doctor and took his hand. The Doctor seemed wary.

"But President! I came all the way from Cruztik, I can't come back tomorrow. I have my work there. We're burning land now. It's a long trip."

The Doctor looked at Salvador, not understanding what he said.

"You've come back then," said Oso, addressing the Mexican.

"That's right."

"Welcome."

"Thank you."

"And where's your man Mario? Or did you fire him?"

The Doctor coughed and took out cigarettes. "Mario's there in the infirmary. None of this was his fault." Oso took the cigarette Méndez offered, but Eliseo refused.

"Good," said Oso.

"But I think we might talk to the Maestro, if you will call him over."

Oso considered this. "Maybe you should talk to the Maestro yourself."

The Doctor put his hands on his hips. "Well, we have to reach some agreement, which you should hear."

"You Institute people have your own affairs, and I have mine to deal with. There's no reason to mix them."

Eliseo wished he could read the Doctor's face, better, wished he knew more about the man, for it looked at first as though the Doctor were going to get angry. Then he seemed to swallow all of his feelings.

"Well enough, President. I'll talk to him sometime."

"Did you lose many teeth?" asked Oso.

"Two."

"And does it hurt?"

"When I make love."

Oso laughed, and Eliseo laughed with him. The corners of the Doctor's mustache turned slightly. He bid Oso good-by, and together the three walked out to the plaza. Eliseo expected the Doctor would go to the school, but instead he went out again into the hot sun toward the infirmary.

"President." The man Salvador had also followed. "Listen to me."

"All right, come with me then, I'm going to urinate."

Oso turned and strode the length of the porch toward Don Concepción's house, down some steps and through a doorway which gave onto a small field behind the Cabildo which the officials used. Excrement and flies were everywhere and the smell was strong. Oso found a bush and turned his back on Salvador. Eliseo stepped up beside Oso and also turned his back.

"I'm poor, President," said Salvador.

"I'm sorry for you." Oso glanced up at the sky.

"You're my brother-in-law."

"I'm sorry for you," Oso repeated.

Eliseo smiled.

Finished, Oso shook himself, straightened his cotton pants and his tunic and turned back to Salvador. "But if you aren't in the Center here in a week ready to assume your work, I'll send the Mayores and the scribes for you, and you'll go to jail."

"But you said before that you'd change my name on the list."

"That was before I became President."

"But Juan—"

"I'm not talking any more about this. Leave us alone now."

The man Salvador sighed, and then bowed to Oso. Oso smiled and touched his brother-in-law lightly on the head with the flat of his right hand.

"You see," he said when the other man had gone, "the world is made up of favors, which you can give or not."

Eliseo nodded. "But why don't you give them?"

"Favors don't always repay," Oso said. "Your father never knew that." He began walking back toward the Cabildo, and put his arm on Eliseo's shoulders. "No, Eliseo, he didn't know that favors just drain from a man's strength."

"Do you like being President?" Eliseo asked.

"It's hard work."

"But do you like it?"

"More than some things I've done."

Juan López Oso went back in the Cabildo to finish working on the conscription release with Don Concepción, and Eliseo went back to reopen Jacinto's store, to play his Mexican guitar and eat his lunch.

18   Mario

HE WAITED ON THE SIDE
of the hill and watched them coming. Both of the men
were drunk, and once José, who carried the rifle, tripped
and almost fell.

When they were close enough to him, Mario offered his
excuse. "I was looking for my sheep."

"You were coming to rob," Miguel said.

"Get off!"

"Pardon me," Mario whispered, "but my children were
bringing the sheep home yesterday, and they said two
men took them away. I don't know what men."

"You aren't allowed on this land," said José.

"No." Mario shook his head, feeling sick. "You're wrong.
Juan López Oso, your brother, has said my sheep may
cross his land going to the pastures, if they don't stop to
graze there."

"But this isn't my brother's land any more."

Mario didn't know what to say. "Do you have my
sheep?" he asked finally.

The two Indians dressed as Ladinos looked at each
other. "Those sheep belong to Don Alonso now, it was
your son who stole them," said José, rubbing at the slight
mustache on his upper lip.

"No." Mario shook his head in denial. Inside he was
angry, but since he could say nothing, his anger became
a kind of pain in his stomach.

"I will talk to the President," he said weakly.

"Juan?" Both men laughed when Miguel spoke. "Juan
will say who they belong to."

"I'll ask," Mario repeated.

"Go ahead," Miguel said.

They would have continued talking to him since they were drunk, but Mario had nothing to say, so he turned and started walking down into the cleft that separated this piece of land from his own. He was halfway down when José called.

"Where's your Paludismo man?"

Mario turned and grinned. "He went away."

He had been hoping that José was so drunk he had forgotten. He had been hoping for a thousand different possibilities.

There was a gully at the bottom of the hill with reeds growing in it. It ran along the bottom land almost to the road, where there was an open plot of sand and then a bridge of logs where the road crossed the gully. Mario came here almost every day to relieve himself, and in the rainy season to pull his sheep out of the mud.

He took a last look at the two men to be sure they were still on the ridge. Then he jumped down in the gully to crouch and run. They were still there.

Mario ran clumsily, as though he were not made for running. His legs remained bent, so with each step his hat showed above the reeds and he dodged the clumps of grass instead of staying close to the sheered-off drop of the hill.

It would sound like someone shooting a rabbit he had been lucky enough to find on his land. Mario's mother would think that, and the dogs at his father's house would bark as though this was all that had happened. Maruch, of course, would know better, and soon would send the oldest son, not for Mario, that would be too dangerous, but by a roundabout path through the bushes to tell

Mario's father. So it would be someone from his father's house who would come first.

They caught him when he reached the open patch before the little bridge. It was not José who shot, but Miguel, since José was not so good with a gun, and begged Miguel to do it for him. From the way the head snapped, it seemed they got him through the neck. They decided to go down and check, but the dogs from a house beyond the road came racing out, and there might be a man with the dogs. So the two men turned and sauntered down their side of the ridge.

19 The Curer

IN THE MIDDLE OF THE night he was asleep happily in a little chair, leaning against the arm of Mario's father, who was also asleep. His bandanna had fallen from around his head and covered his eyes.

Money that was dropped on the dead man's chest clinked and woke him up. The newcomer told Mario's father they could not find anyone to say the prayers. Mario's father turned to the curer.

"Will you say the prayers?" he asked.

"Look." The curer grabbed the old man's arm at the wrist. "I was just going by on the road, and I heard the music from the harp and the guitar, so I came to see what was wrong. I can't say the prayers, I'm very drunk."

"But no one else will say them." Mario's father sniffed and wiped his nose with the back of his free hand.

"You are better now," the curer said. "I can tell it from what your blood is saying."

"Will you say prayers? Please?"

"Much better. Your soul is all there."

Mario's father sniffed again and spat on the floor, near the body.

The harp player and his son who played the guitar were tuning their instruments, carefully, slowly, each silver plunk followed by a scraping noise as the wooden pegs were wound a bit.

Mario's father began to cry again, and the curer patted his arm.

"Won't you do it?" the father asked.

The curer pushed his bandanna back on his head, and thought for a moment. Then he searched for a flea that was biting him.

"Look at that child!" he said finally. A little boy in the dark back corner of the smoky room was pulling on the cat's tail. The cat was howling.

The curer rolled off his chair and half walked, half crawled through the sitting men and sleeping women to where the child was.

At last the music began again, drowning the sounds of the wife crying and the laughter of the neighbors who were outside in the early morning half-light, drunk.

One of the women murmured that the chicken was ready, and her helpers began passing bowls and getting tortillas for the men to eat.

When he had eaten, Mario's father remembered they had not prayed yet. He stumbled outside, could not find the curer, and stumbled back inside. Mario's son Antun finally found the man, asleep under the bed with the cat sleeping beside him. He had pulled all of the old sandals and pieces of trash and useless cloth around him so no one would find him. Mario's father took a candle to look at the curer, but the man was smiling in his sleep and Mario's father decided to say the prayers himself, if he could remember them.

20   The Maestro

DOCTOR MÉNDEZ stopped by a fat old Indian lady with thinning hair and bought some tortillas from her. The tortillas were in a deep basket and covered with a cloth. She dug down and counted out five tortillas that were still warm. The Doctor thanked her in Spanish she did not understand, and he went on down the line of women sitting on the ground in the plaza, to a place where there was a pot of coffee boiling over a smoky little fire. When he pointed, the woman tending the coffee gave him a glassful which was thick and hot. He stood while eating his breakfast, and continued looking around the Sunday market for his assistant Mario.

The boy was usually reliable, and the Doctor wondered why he had not returned when he said he would. As a rule they always opened the infirmary on Sunday.

Eliseo was standing in front of Jacinto's store watching the market, his hands deep in the pockets of the Mexican jacket he wore over his tunic. Scribes were going from vendor to vendor collecting taxes. The morning sun was thin, the day cold and windy.

Juan López Oso came out of his store, carrying his silver-headed cane. He was hatless, as usual, and for a moment his great shock of black hair ruffled like a coxcomb. Oso picked his way between the seated women and their little stacks of goods for sale, and passed close to the Doctor. Not stopping he called out good morning in Spanish and went on his way to the Cabildo.

The Doctor was warmed by his coffee and filled by the tortillas, and worried about what illness he would get from eating them. He walked over to the front gates of the church of San Juan. No sign of the priest there, his motorbike wasn't anywhere in sight. Sometimes the padre came out from San Martín to say the Mass, but more often he didn't make it.

Eliseo had begun playing records on the loud-speaker and for long seconds the music would come out loud. Then the wind would whip around and the sound from the loud-speaker would be almost indistinguishable from the murmur of the market.

The Doctor wandered over to Jacinto's store and offered Eliseo a cigarette. The boy took one, and the Doctor offered a match. Méndez stood a moment, still searching the market with his eyes for Mario.

"I told your father once that he was sick, but he didn't believe me," the Doctor said.

Eliseo said nothing.

"I was sorry about it anyway."

Like his father, Eliseo had a kind of refinement and delicacy. His bones were thin, his cheeks high, his eyes almost slits. Already Eliseo looked old and sage. But his mouth was wide, and when he smiled he looked more like an idiot, thought Méndez.

"Have you seen Mario?" he asked.

"No."

Eliseo went inside the store. Méndez followed and found Eliseo opening a bottle of beer.

"Will you drink one of these, Señor?" Eliseo asked.

"It's too early in the morning."

"Go ahead, it's already open."

The Doctor took the bottle and saluted Eliseo. "Here," he said, digging into his pocket for change, "let me buy you one."

"All right." Eliseo took another bottle from the shelf behind the counter, opened it and efficiently swept the peso the Doctor had put on the counter into a drawer.

"You know, Señor, my father drank too much. When my mother died he drank every day."

Méndez nodded, and leaned back against the counter. Overhead on a string were smelly dried fish which Eliseo sold for a peso or two, and strands of candles in all different colors, shapes and sizes. These were sold to Indians on their way to pray in the church, Mario had told the Doctor once.

"Can I go out back?" the Doctor asked when he finished his beer.

"Of course."

While the Doctor was gone, relieving himself, the Maestro came into the store, not yet quite awake. His hair was rumpled and there was still sleep in his eyes.

"Your friend is here," Eliseo announced when the Maestro came in.

"Mario?"

"No." Eliseo smiled. "The Doctor. Do you want one of these?" He took down a beer without waiting for an answer.

The Maestro drank, and nodded toward the back of the

store. "What's he want here anyway?" he asked in a low voice.

"Looking for Mario."

"Have you seen him? I was looking for him too."

The Doctor came back in the store, closing the door quietly behind himself. The Maestro pretended not to notice the other Mexican.

"I don't think Mario is coming today," Eliseo said.

"Why not?" the Doctor asked.

"They say he died."

"Who says that?" asked the Maestro.

"Some people. They were in Lumtik yesterday, and said they saw Mario's father putting him in the ground."

It was a possibility, thought the Maestro, chilling, almost unbelievable. The Center was the place of rumors and lies and mistakes.

"Do you know what happened?" asked the Doctor, putting his hands on his hips.

"No. He died. They said he had been shot with a gun."

The Maestro thought of Mario's hamlet. He tried to picture a man there who had a shotgun, who would mistake Mario for a trespasser. But he couldn't see it. The hamlet in his mind was all peace—cooing women drawing water, men shouting "brother" to each other as they passed through their neighbors' fields.

"I'll go there to his house and find out," the Maestro said.

"All right," said Eliseo.

The Maestro had hoped that when he said he was going Eliseo would finally put an end to the joke. But instead Eliseo's eyes only narrowed and his face seemed to tighten, the thin skin stretching more over the obvious bones.

The Maestro turned to the Doctor. "Are you going to come?"

The Doctor considered. "No. There's no reason to."

"That's right, there's no reason for you," the Maestro said.

He shook hands with Eliseo and thanked him for the beer, and went out into the market. As he walked out of the plaza on the road by the Cabildo, he turned several times to look back, on the chance he had somehow been fooled and Eliseo was coming to tell him. When he was halfway out of the valley he could hear Eliseo playing Mexican records—*Jalisco, Jalisco is my beloved home*—as if nothing had really happened.

If there was danger, thought the Maestro, it was probably his own fault. He could remember going outside early in the morning when he was staying at Mario's house, while Maruch was busy grinding corn, and Mario was sitting on the bed by the fire, dressed, but quietly catching an extra nap before breakfast, with his eyes closed, his hands clasped between his knees. The Maestro would go outside, cold at first. The sun would be barely over the hills in the east, shining behind the great crosses of San Pedro which stood above the village. Below in the valley, mist remained in the hollows like pools of thin milk. The path, twisting down below Mario's house, would be wet and slick, steaming in the places where the sun hit it. From time to time a family or a pair of women would come over the brow of the hill and pad down, carrying eggs to San Martín. Or a lone woman in black with a heavy net bag full of charcoal on her back and a bunch of red gladiolas teetering on her head. Some people, not in such a great rush to get to San Martín, would notice the Maestro, and stop to stare at him. Once in a while a man would call out good morning in Spanish, and the Maestro would reply, amazed each time how a soft voice would carry so well over the stillness. The man would readjust the rope of his tumpline, or the weight on his back, and would go on, running to make up the time he had lost when he stopped to talk. Then there might be a soft voice in the house, Mario instructing Maruch, and she would appear at the doorway, smiling. She would come out beside the Maestro, and ask him who was going by. Just a man, he would say, and she would laugh, and then go back inside to tell Mario.

It occurred to the Maestro now that his presence in their house might be a cause of concern for them. Strangers might not know he meant no harm. There was always the possibility, the Maestro knew, that someone might think he was a witch, and might think Mario a protector of witches.

Before, the Maestro had thought of this rare chance as a danger to himself. He had not thought what it might do to Mario.

Once over the hill of San Pedro, he passed a few stragglers coming late to the market. As each white-dressed man came into sight from a distance he hoped it was Mario. But then, even before the man got close enough for the Maestro to see his face, something in the gait, in the way the man ran down a certain incline or took to one side of a rutted part of the road instead of the other, told the Mexican this one could not be his friend.

The wind was out of the north and pushing him along. He thought again of his own danger. The same man who had shot Mario as a keeper of witches would be there to take some shots at him. At first the possibility caught in his throat, and he was afraid. Then, because he was almost

running, sweat broke out on his face, and came cold under
his arms beneath his jacket, and he wasn't thinking of the
man with the gun any more.

Coming out of the last of the brown cornfields, he
crossed the little open patch by the house of Mario's
father. The house was closed up and barred, not even a
telltale wisp of smoke escaped under the eaves. The Maestro called in Tzotzil, but got no answer. The dogs were
gone from the yard, and even listening carefully he could
not hear anything move inside. None of the usual pots and
drying pieces of clothing lay strewn about the yard. It was
as if the house and all that belonged to it were drawn in
against him. He had the feeling that there were people
inside, but he couldn't be sure.

From the path below Mario's he looked up at his friend's
house. No one was there, except one of the dogs, which
began barking frantically when the Maestro came up to
the house. The sheep were gone, and the chickens. But
this house seemed almost inviting. Both doors were open.
The Mexican went inside, and found it barren. Everything
that could be moved, except the stones around the fireplace, was gone—the crosses, the big jars for storing corn,
all the firewood, Maruch's utensils. The planks which
made up the bed had been taken, and only the stakes
which had supported it remained. It was as cold inside
the house as outside, and the Maestro bent down to the
fireplace and felt in the ashes for warmth. Nothing. The
Maestro went outside again.

Up by the father's house he saw something move. He
was convinced it was the killer, though the movement was
slight enough to be just a bush rattling in the wind. He
started to duck, when the figure moved again, around the

corner of the father's house. Recognizing it, the Maestro broke into a trot.

"Father," he called out softly. There was no answer, and he called again. He came up closer and saw the door was slightly ajar. Another dog, this one white, had joined the black one from Mario's house, and they circled behind the Ladino, growling and sniffing.

"Father?"

The voice of the old man inside barely carried to the Maestro. "What is it?" he said in Tzotzil.

"I've come."

"You've come."

Usually there was a kind of pleased satisfaction in that statement. When Mario's father said it, it was dead. The Maestro went to the door. The father was alone, sitting on a tiny chair by the fireplace. On the floor beside him was a bundle of sticks, and he was feeding them one by one into the single little flame before him.

The Maestro pushed against the door and squeezed inside. This house was cold too. The old man did not look up from his work.

"He died then?" asked the teacher in Spanish.

The father nodded, and slowly got up. He moved the chair he had been sitting on into place for his guest, and reached out for a stool for himself. He indicated the younger man was to sit down.

The father looked tired, but otherwise no different, thought the Maestro.

"How?" he asked.

"A man with a gun," said the father in slow Spanish, going back to his work of feeding the flame.

Inadvertently, the Maestro reached out to warm his

hands over the fire. His moving hands seemed to startle the old man.

"Who?"

"A *hkashlan*."

"Huh!" The Maestro let breath escape in a little sigh of recognition the way Indians did.

Then maybe the death was not my fault, he thought.

"Do you know the man?"

Mario's father paused, a twig he had been about to break bowed in his hand. "Yes."

"Who is it?"

"A man who works for Don Alonso," the old man said slowly, softly, speaking the Spanish he had almost forgotten in a high voice, halting between words.

"I'm sorry, Father."

The old man broke his twig and tossed it at the fire, and then nodded again in agreement.

"Where are Maruch and the children?" the Mexican asked in Tzotzil.

"They went away to her mother's house."

"They're going to live there?"

"Yes."

The schoolteacher felt for his cigarettes in his jacket and brought out the pack. The old man took one, thanking him, and got a flaming twig from the fire to light for both of them. He inhaled several times and then spat and held the cigarette close to his face so the smoke columned up on either side of his nose, and eventually made his eyes wet.

"Did you tell the new President?"

"This Oso?"

"Yes."

The old man shut his eyes and shook his head—no.

"But, Father, he will go to San Martín and have them put the man who killed Mario in jail."

Again the old man shook his head. "No, it was on Oso's land he was killed."

The Mexican did not quite understand, though he realized that Oso was therefore involved somehow. They smoked on, as the old man built up his fire. Now it was warm inside the house.

"Do you know this Ladino, Don Roberto, in town?" the Maestro asked finally.

"Yes, of course."

"Go to him, and tell him."

Again the old man shook his head.

"Why not?" asked the Maestro. The original tension had slaked off him, and a new one, akin to anger, was coming.

"Why?" asked the father, in Spanish.

The young man did not have his reasons ready. "Are you too old and tired to go, Father?"

"Yes." The man's eyes were barely open.

"Then I'll go."

"No, don't do that."

"But Don Roberto is your friend, isn't he?"

The father hesitated, just a second, and then seemed to raise his whole body up and down as he agreed.

"It would do no good," he said slowly.

The Maestro stood up. For a few minutes he had been lulled by the old man's kindness to him. Now he felt distant again, on the other side of the fence. He took money, thirty pesos, from his pocket, and held it out. "Can you give this to Maruch? I'll come again when I have more."

"No," said the father.

The Maestro thought the old man was saying no to the money, and then that he was saying no to the promise to come again.

"I'm sorry, Father, in my heart," he said in Tzotzil.

"Why?"

"He was my friend. He was a good man."

"Yes," the old man agreed.

"I have to go, Father."

"Go on, then."

The Mexican bowed to the old man and kept his head down. For a second nothing happened, and then he felt the touch of the father's whole hand against his head, and he straightened up.

"I'm going," he said, pulling open the door. There was nothing else to say in Tzotzil, and he started out.

"Go with God," the old man said softly in Spanish.

Outside the Maestro repeated this.

He still had the money in his hand, so he turned and found a path down to the road. Continuing along it, past the ravine where the waterhole for the hamlet lay, he came to the house of Maruch's mother, a small one which often stood open and served as a store and a bar. Now the doors were closed, but smoke seeped out through the straw on the roof.

The Maestro remembered what Maruch had said. If Mario came home with another wife she would take her pot and her children and go home to her mother's house.

He called "I've come" from the road, and got no reply. He had not actually expected one. He called Maruch's name, and roused one of the dogs sleeping behind the house.

Mario's father knew the Maestro was not responsible,

Maruch must know it too. Yet maybe they knew he was not responsible for the act itself, and still would not dissociate him from all that had happened.

He called again and waited. He thought of all the times he had called "I've come" and Maruch had shown her delight. You've come. And then once inside, Manvel repeating the whole thing. You've come.

He had turned away, prepared to go back to the village, when Pascual, probably unseen by those inside, came darting out the back door and ran down to the fence.

"Maestro!"

The Mexican returned and lifted the little boy off the fence. For a minute he held the child up, and then took him onto his hip. Pascual straddled easily.

There was little they could say to one another.

"My father died."

"I know. That's a pity." *Lastimó.*

The boy nodded. He held tight around the Mexican's neck with one hand.

"I'm sad in my heart," said the Maestro.

The boy nodded again, solemnly.

"Here, this is a gift for your mother. To buy food." He handed the money to the boy. Pascual crumpled it and held it in his free hand.

"Are you going to sleep here?" Pascual asked.

"No, I'm going back to the village." He let the boy down.

"Go on then."

Pascual climbed up on the gate to watch the Maestro go. He still had three ten-peso bills in his hand.

Walking back to the village the Maestro told himself that he was a realist and that men died every day. But when he saw the Center again from the hill, he forgot all that, and to his embarrassment he began to cry as he came down into the valley.

When he got to Jacinto's store and was safe inside with Eliseo, he wiped his eyes on the sleeve of his jacket, and explained it away by saying the wind was quite strong. Eliseo brought a bottle of trago, and poured a glass for the Maestro. The Mexican drank.

"What about Mario?" asked Eliseo.

"He's dead, you were right. He was killed by a Mexican, on Oso's land. Shot."

"Yes, that's what they said."

The Maestro sat down at the table in the store. He was winded from his walk to Lumtik, and from the morning itself. The liquor Eliseo had given him was making him confused.

Eliseo went to the corner by the front door and fumbled with the two plugs which connected the car battery to the record player and loud-speaker. The plugs hissed and sparked, then the red eye below the turntable lit and Eliseo selected a record. The scratching of the needle was amplified a hundred times in the market and in the store, making the Maestro jump, and then the mariachi band, all violins and thump-thump, began to grind out a tune.

"Here, have some more." Eliseo brought the bottle and the glass to the teacher and poured another drink.

He could barely hear Eliseo over the boom of the record player.

"Are you sad, then?"

"What?"

"Are you sad—about Mario?" the boy persisted.

"Yes!"

"Sadder than about the old President?"

The Maestro didn't know what to answer. He didn't know what he felt. The comparison of griefs had not occurred to him before.

He was very tired, he knew, and his eyes stung as if he had been crying longer than he actually had been.

"I don't know."

They drank again, quickly.

"I don't have money to pay for this," said the teacher at last, pointing at the bottle. The thirty pesos he had given to Pascual earlier was all the money he had.

"No, I don't want it. This is a gift to you." Eliseo placed the remainder of the clear liquid in front of the Mexican. "Here in Chomtik, a man should drink when he's sad in his heart." Eliseo spoke as though reciting an old rule.

"Eliseo, I'm very sad."

The record had ended, and its amplified scratching sent a pulse shivering through the store. But Eliseo did not go to turn it off. He seemed oblivious to all distractions, and yet also removed from what was going on between himself and the Mexican.

When he finally got up to turn off the machine, Eliseo stopped and stretched in the doorway.

"What are you going to do now?" The innocent look had resettled on Eliseo's little face.

"I don't know. I'm going to pour you a drink, if this is really my bottle."

Eliseo dismissed the bottle with a slight wave of his hand. "It's yours."

The Maestro felt for the bottle and poured the glass brim full.

"Thank you," Eliseo said. He took the glass and held it lightly in his hand, staring down.

"Drink!" demanded the Maestro in Tzotzil.

"All right."

Eliseo's speed and precision were startling. In a single move he downed the drink, and reached for the bottle so he could pour for the Maestro.

The Maestro began wagging his head from side to side, until the room began to turn and made him sick. Slowly he got up and wandered around the store to clear his head. But he came too close to the dead smell of the dried fish hanging over the counter, and this made him sick again, so he sat down.

"I'm going to talk to Don Roberto—the lawyer—you know him?"

"Yes. My father was his friend." A little pride showed in Eliseo's face.

"About getting the man who killed Mario."

"You shouldn't go to Don Roberto," Eliseo said.

"Why not?"

"Because you're drunk."

The Maestro said, "I'll go when I'm sober."

"You shouldn't—that's the business of the village, of the President."

"Oso?"

"Yes."

"I'll see him, then." The teacher got up, slowly again. Somehow the fear which Mario's father had shown when Oso's name was mentioned had kept this possibility from the Maestro's mind. Now Eliseo showed the same hesitancy and looked for a moment as if he would block the doorway when the Maestro headed for it.

"Is he at the Cabildo?"

"I don't know." Eliseo was sullen.

The Indians could not understand a Mexican's insistence. They could be put off by any hindrance, any mere gesture at refusal. The path of least resistance for them, the Maestro thought.

"I think he's there," he said. "Thank you, Eliseo. Thank you for the *posh.*"

"Just a little *posh.*"

"Strong, though."

Eliseo could not help smiling, he had been complimented on his hospitality.

Lightly, the Maestro took the boy's hand, shook it and left.

He crossed through the market, going slow and being careful to avoid stepping in the wares of the women.

The officials were sitting close together for warmth on the wooden benches flanking the doors of the Cabildo. Huddled to themselves against the cold, their hands inside their tunics, they looked sad to him.

Oso was inside, smoking a cigarette, sitting on the edge of a table and looking at the pictures in an old Mexico City newspaper. His cane of office was tucked under one arm.

With admirable industry, Don Concepción pecked away at the typewriter, his chins tucked down, disappearing into the collar of his jacket. Though Don Concepción looked up from his work and smiled, Oso pretended he had not seen the Maestro come in.

"President." The Maestro stepped up to Oso and bowed his head. Quickly, Oso released him with the back of his hand.

"I was in Lumtik this morning, President," the Maestro said in Spanish. "What they said is true."

"What's that?"

"Mario López Gomez was killed."

Don Concepción looked up. He had heard the rumor himself, but had not believed it. The old man wagged his head, thinking this new development was a pity. And so soon after the Indians had settled down again following the old President's death.

"Do they have the body?" Oso asked.

"No, his father buried it yesterday," said the Maestro.

"Then we don't know if it's true or not, do we? Maybe he died, just died. Or maybe this Mario ran away to hot country because he owed money." Oso took up his paper again, pretending he was going to read.

They were dancing, or circling each other, or maybe, under the civility of their slow, articulate Spanish, they were grappling. The Maestro could not tell. But he was scared, and wished he had not felt duty bound a few minutes ago to bring on this scene.

"His father, the past president, said he was shot by a Mexican on the land next to Mario's own." The Mexican did not have the courage to say *on your land.*

"The past president is very old." Oso dropped the pretense of reading his Mexican newspaper and used his silver cane to tap gently at his own temple.

Both Don Concepción and the Maestro understood him, of course. The Maestro was sure that Don Concepción didn't believe Oso either, but the Secretary was discreet.

"They say in Lumtik he was shot with a gun by a Mexican. By a *hkashlan.*"

" 'They say in Lumtik,' Maestro. How could that be? The land next to Mario's is my own." Oso put the paper down on the table. "And there are no Mexicans on my land for sure."

The Maestro looked at his feet. The argument was lop-sided. All the truths available were Oso's, so he couldn't fight any more. "Well, President," he said, smiling, and considering himself a true drunken coward, "I'm going."

"Where?"

"To San Martín." The Maestro paused. "I have negocios in town." A man's business—his negocios—was his own, a kind of inviolable excuse and secret a man could keep to himself. Even the President couldn't touch these. "Until later, President."

The Maestro tried not to be overly contemptuous, yet he remembered when he got outside on the stone porch that instead of bowing to Oso as he had done when he came in, he only offered his hand on leaving. But the breech was not wide open yet, for Oso had returned the handshake.

21   Miguel

JUAN LÓPEZ OSO WAS sitting near the fire in the rear of his own store, his hands hanging between his spread knees. He stared at the patch of gray cold morning which showed through the doorway, and then shifted to watching his wife as she warmed tortillas from the day before over the fire. Snug between two smoldering logs was a pot of beans, bubbling slightly as a head of brown juice turned to froth and edged over the lip of the pot.

The woman knew when she was being watched, and

she moved carefully, dusting ash from each tortilla as she took it off the fire and flipped it into a gourd bowl. Something she was doing was wrong and would bring on his anger, but she couldn't decide what.

Oso spat a whispered order for water and the woman sprang up, took a bowl with her and went outside to fetch it for him. He swished the water around several times in the bowl before he drank from it, so she understood the water was too dirty. She waited, watching him, as he forced the water between his teeth and spat carefully on the floor. Then he put the bowl down, scooped up water and ran his hands through his long, coarse hair. Again he spat.

"More, hot now."

She took back the bowl and pushed another pot closer to the fire, to warm the water.

Oso was not used to sleeping on the floor any more, he wasn't a child, and his discomfort after a bad night showed as he tried to find a new way to sit on his low chair.

"We'll eat now," he said finally. Then he got up and went to the figure sleeping under the wool blankets on the bed in the corner.

"Brother," he said. "Miguel—we'll eat now." Gently, he tugged at the blanket, uncovering his brother's thin, sagging face.

Miguel opened his eyes.

"Come on, it's late. It's seven o'clock."

"God damn it." Miguel was awake, but he turned away from his brother to steal some more sleep.

"Come on." Oso laughed.

"Late for goddamn Indians," Miguel said deliberately, resentful as he threw off the blankets and sat up on the side of the bed to rub his face and his eyes into action.

Miguel had tumbled into the bed the night before, drunk, in all his clothes, and now he stood up and tucked his dirty white shirt into his pants. Juan and the woman watched him, and he put his hand inside his pants to scratch.

"Fleas," Miguel explained.

His brother didn't venture an answer.

"A little cruda, huh, Juan?" Miguel put his hand on his brother's shoulder. "Well, they say Indians shouldn't drink."

Juan shrugged, and his brother's hand fell away. He thought of the other saying—Mexicans shouldn't drink with Indians.

Miguel sat down on the other little chair by the fire and rubbed his hands together. "Well, what is it? Beans and tortillas and coffee?"

The woman nodded, and passed the gourd bowl of tortillas to her husband.

"In the name of God—" Miguel began, but suddenly broke off in the middle, and let out a fitful small laugh.

"What?"

"Nothing." Miguel looked up at the woman.

"You were going to say I eat like an Indian, isn't that it?"

"Well—" Miguel shrugged.

Oso let the gourd bowl drop and it rolled away toward the fire. He stood up, not taking his eyes from his brother —Miguel was afraid—and then Oso went to the front of the store and started taking things off the shelf. Though they couldn't see him Miguel and the woman could judge his angry movements. He returned in a second and threw a package of crackers toward the woman's lap. He fumbled with his knife as he came, gouging holes in the lid of a big can of salted fish. The juice spurted out onto his tunic.

"Here," he said, holding the can under his brother's face, and ripping back the tin with his hand. Then he dropped the can and stalked out the front door.

Miguel, full of spiced salmon and tortillas and coffee, found his brother an hour later, sitting beside the stream which ran out from a waterhole near the ascent toward San Pedro. The bank of the stream was thick with good grass, and ten feet away some young women were washing clothes in the water. When Miguel arrived, Juan pretended he had not seen his older brother coming. He had taken off his sandals and was rubbing the dirt from one of his wet legs.

Miguel crouched in the grass beside him and waited.

"Do you think it's going to rain then?" asked Miguel as though they were in the middle of a talk.

"No, the clouds are going away over there behind the church." Oso deliberately put his clean foot back in the water, and began work on the other.

Miguel sat down, took off his sandals and put his feet into the water beside his brother's. He had brought his leather bag with him and from it he took a ten-peso bottle of sweet vermouth.

"Will you drink with me, then, Brother?" he asked, holding the bottle out so Juan had to take it.

"What for?"

"I feel a little sick in my head, in my stomach, so I want to drink this. A little sick from so much *posh* last night."

"And from too much spiced fish this morning." Oso took the bottle.

Miguel could feel the opening, and took it, laughing. Juan laughed too, and twisted the cap off the bottle.

"Here," said Juan, "drink."

"No, go ahead, you need it more than I do." Miguel smiled and rubbed his feet together in the water.

"Last night you said you didn't have any money left. Where did you get this?" asked Juan when they had both drunk two or three swallows of the vermouth. He spoke quietly, since he could feel that the girls washing clothes were trying to hear what he was saying. Their giggles gave them away.

"I borrowed this Torino from the store of the President of Chomtik—he wasn't there, but since he's a rich man and my friend, I knew he would be glad to help a poor Ladino."

"The President of Chomtik doesn't feel very warm in his heart toward Ladinos," said Oso, passing the bottle back to his brother.

"But he *will* drink with them, won't he?"

"The saying is that Mexicans shouldn't drink with Indians." Oso took his feet from the water and brought his knees up to his chest.

The girls were through with their work, the washed clothes were tied in bundles and waiting on the bank, and now one by one each girl lifted her black skirt and stepped into the stream, bent over and let the water run through her hair, then climbed back on the bank and took out a comb. At once the light laughter increased.

"You know a woman is bad when she talks too much," Oso said to his brother in a loud voice.

As if his breath was the wind, the girls took flight on it. Combs disappeared, the bundles were lifted, the girls left, and the men were alone.

"Why isn't the President of Chomtik hearing cases this morning, making agreements, making money?"

Oso placed the bottle between them on the grass. "Today the President is helping his Ladino friend."

"But Brother, does a Ladino need help from any Indian, even the President?" Miguel smirked.

"Only if the Ladino is crazy and in trouble."

They thought about that as they watched an old man with gray hair knocking his way down the path from San Pedro with a heavy load of firewood on his back. When he got near them the old man lifted his hat and called out "President." Oso nodded and the old man went on.

As Oso had predicted, the clouds began to thin behind the church and the pale form of the sun became visible, slowly heating the valley. The day began to take on a metallic sheen, which it would hold unless the wind came in the afternoon.

"But Ladinos are smarter than that, aren't they, Miguel?" Oso pursued his question. His brother was lying back on the grass, shielding his eyes with his arm.

"No."

"Then what can a poor Indian do? Even a President? Here, drink."

Miguel sat up, took the bottle, drank some of the sweet stuff with the tart edge like lime, and blinked as he opened his eyes. "Don't worry, Juan, nothing will happen," he said.

Oso wondered at this strength in his brother's manner, since it had not been there the day before when Miguel first came to him with the story—already half drunk, looking as though he had been crying, his eyes almost caked shut, his long face pale and twisted.

Both brothers lay back, the bottle between them, their feet dangling in the water.

Oso slept comfortably for a while, a vague smile on his

mouth. He woke once, turned his head and saw the sharp profile of his brother. Miguel's face was different, the paler skin pulled tight over the high nose; the eyes when closed were barely shielded by the lids and the skin there fluttered and jerked so it was always impossible to tell if Miguel was really asleep or just thinking.

It reminded Oso of another time, when they were both young, in their twenties. Miguel had gone away to hot country to work as a picker in a huge coffee plantation called La Grita, where they paid Indians eight pesos a day. Miguel had been gone almost a year. Nothing had been heard from him—he sent no money—and Juan began to think his brother had disappeared for good. He wondered if he should make the journey down to Arriaga, especially since he should tell his brother that their father had died soon after the fiesta of San Mateo. Then one day some men passed through Lumtik on their way home from the fincas, dirty, bedraggled and sick from the long stay in hot country. Oso confronted them on the road, brought them to his house and gave them water and then corn gruel, which they accepted. When men returned from fincas, it was a homecoming even with strangers they did not know. Oso sat quietly with them, letting them talk in their pale voices about the conditions and the work in the plantations. At last he could contain himself no longer and asked if they had seen Miguel anywhere. No, they said— then they thought. But there was a man of that name at La Grita, who some other men said was sick.

As soon as the men had gone, struggling into the last few hours of their trip, Oso began hurriedly to make preparations for his own journey, and early the next morning he left for Arriaga, light and relieved since the hardest part of the business—the decision to go—had been made.

He found La Grita by asking—everyone in hot country seemed to know where the great finca was—and one of the Mexican overseers in the office there sent a boy with Oso to the grand barracks where the Indians slept and where Miguel was lying sick.

Miguel was almost yellow when Oso found him on a cot halfway down the hall where a hundred men slept at night. It was one of the tropical diseases, passing now, but still Miguel's thinned body shook from time to time. They no longer paid him, but the overseer had allowed him to stay on until he was better, and the other men were feeding him with tortillas they took from their own dinner. The younger brother was allowed to stay too, in the next cot, until Miguel was well enough to leave.

They did not talk the first day, but some time during the night one of the chill spells came on Miguel and he reached out a cold, wet hand and grabbed his brother's arm in the dark.

"Why did you come?" he asked in a hoarse whisper. All around them the men were asleep in the heat of the shed, turning and moving in the thick air.

"You were sick," Oso answered, fully awake.

Miguel clutched his arm tighter. "What more?"

"The father died."

"When?"

"After San Mateo. There's land for you, I came to tell you."

Around them other men moved, disturbed in their sleep by the noise. Miguel lay back, and after a while the chill seemed to go and Miguel relaxed, though his hold on his brother's arm remained tight.

"I won't take the land; do you want it?"

"I can't," Oso said warily. "It's ejido, I can't take it." He tried to persuade Miguel to come back, but Miguel lay still, his eyelids flickering.

"Look," Miguel said. "Buy the land from me."

"Why?"

"I owe men here six hundred pesos and I can't leave."

Oso understood then why his brother had not risked the trip home even though he was sick.

The younger brother never asked where the money had gone—drinking, gambling, theft probably—but if Miguel owed it to the Mexican overseers and sneaked away, they would find him, even in Chomtik, and have him put in jail. If he owed it to Indians, they would find him and maybe kill him.

Oso agreed reluctantly to take the land. He did not want it so much, he had just received his own small piece of land and felt like a rich man. But he thought of Miguel's situation as his own, as though they were one man and a burden had suddenly fallen to this man.

In the morning, Oso went to the sweating overseer, who looked at his arms and legs the way a pig trader looks at a possible buy, while Oso explained he would do his brother's work. In the damp early morning he took off his white tunic before the overseer, and showed him his strength. When the overseer agreed Oso went to work twelve hours a day—six to six—picking in the hot sun, ducking into the faintly sweet foliage of the coffee trees to get the beans, but never able to stay long enough where there was any shade. They paid him only seven pesos a day, charging a peso for Miguel's board now there was money for that. But in the second week they let Oso go to work in the cooking shed, where women worked all

night by candle making tortillas. From six until one Oso
ground the corn on a huge hand-powered mill, and for this
the overseer paid him another seven pesos.

From the first few weeks of his work Oso remembered
very little, except the sensation of working only in his cotton drawers and shirt, without his tunic, which made him
feel naked and unprotected. And the press of the cold
dough against his stomach in the night, for he found that
while working the big handle of the mill he could steal
some of the wet masa, and thus avoid having to spend one
of his pesos from each day's work to buy tortillas. When
he came back to the sweltering dormitorio in the middle
of the night, he would wake Miguel and the older brother
would sit up while they shared the dough. Oso would always eat the bad part of it, the stuff which had been
closest to his skin and which smelled like himself.

Toward the end of the three months it took him to
make the money, Miguel's sickness was over. They were
eating in the dark one night, and Oso said they could start
home at the end of the next week—Miguel was well
enough, the money was almost paid off, and they would
have enough left to take a truck as far as San Martín. As
Oso talked, Miguel began to shake his head, and at last
he whispered that he would not be going.

"Are you going to stay in the finca?" Juan could not
understand.

"No, I'll look for work in Arriaga."

"But"—Oso could not believe his brother—"but hot country, it isn't good for Indians. We get sick here, you know
that yourself."

Miguel was silent for a long time. At last he said, "Then
we have to stop being Indians."

Miguel would say nothing more about it, and soon lay

back on his cot and fell into his light sleep. Juan watched his brother that night, and the feelings which came to him were the same as those which came to him years later as they lay together on the bank of the stream letting their feet dangle in the water. The night long ago on the finca La Grita had proved that even though they were brothers they were not the same person. Oso had worked to pay back the money as though it was his own debt, but when this was done the brothers split again. He could see Miguel returning to his own self, and Oso could tell they were two men again. For him it was the feeling a man has when the curer has returned his soul to him.

Oso was not happy when he climbed on the truck for home and Miguel handed him a piece of paper which said all of their father's land was now Juan's—he didn't really care about that. He felt himself again as he left Arriaga, the memory of the heat and the misery of his work on the finca began to fade as the truck from Flores faced the mountain road and the colder climate of San Martín and Chomtik beyond that, but Oso sensed he would almost rather have the closeness of his brother, the kind of sharing which the touching bunks and the debt at La Grita had given them for three months.

Now when Eliseo came up on them and woke them to say Don Roberto had called for the President on the phone from San Martín, Oso looked immediately to his older brother, saw the eyes flash open, and since he knew so well what to look for, Oso saw a flicker of fear coming from inside Miguel. And this fear became Juan's and a bond which made them one brother again. Oso had known such a closeness was going to return but he had fought it, not knowing whether he wanted it. Now that it had come, he took it eagerly and felt strong.

"I won't come with you to the Cabildo," Miguel said in a low voice.

Eliseo waited patiently while Oso got up, dried his feet on the grass, and strapped on his sandals. Then Juan started out toward the road to the plaza and the Cabildo, with Eliseo beside him.

"How are you, President?" Eliseo asked, turning to look up at the other man.

"What do you mean?"

"You were drunk with your brother last night."

"Yes. I'm all right now."

"Do you remember what you did when you came into Jacinto's?" Eliseo was breathing hard, finding it difficult to keep up with Oso's long, loping stride.

"No," Oso said and brushed the hair out of his eyes.

A smile was around the President's mouth, so Eliseo decided the older man did remember.

"You told Jacinto you were going to screw his wife and then screw him."

Oso laughed. "And what did Jacinto say to me then?"

"That your own new wife must not serve you well, then, if she leaves you so hungry!"

They had come to the place where the road fed into the plaza and Oso stopped for a moment, staring across at the long, low, tile-roofed white Cabildo, which ran half the length of the opposite side of the barren plaza.

Eliseo knew what the phone call from Don Roberto in San Martín meant almost as well as Oso did, and he expected that Oso was pausing because he was afraid. But when Eliseo looked up into the other man's face, he saw that Oso was still amused, thinking about something else.

"Jacinto—" Oso said as he started down to cross the plaza, "Jacinto would be a good man if he didn't want to be a Mexican so much." The sharp, rugged, slightly sinister face widened into a fuller smile.

Eliseo thought he had caught Oso. "What is wrong with wanting to become a Mexican, President?" he asked.

"Only the strongest Indians can do it," Oso said, not breaking his stride.

Eliseo turned off from the other man. "I have to watch the store."

"Come on with me, Eliseo, let's see what that son-of-a-whore lawyer in San Martín wants."

Don Concepción was grunting into the old, ornate telephone when Oso and Eliseo walked into the office. "Yes, Don Roberto," he said, "if I take my medicine, then I'll live a long time." He turned and saw Oso, but his baggy old face gave no answer to the question of the meaning of the call. "Here comes the President, Don Roberto."

Oso thought of Don Concepción's respectful, deferential tone as he answered the lawyer's polite question, and Oso forgave the old Secretary. After all, Don Concepción was a viejo, a sick old man, and that explained it.

"Good," said Oso loudly into the telephone. "I'm here." His Spanish was harsh and hurried.

While Don Roberto edged around to the point, saying he had a problem which the President could help him with, Oso dug into the pocket of the shirt he wore under his tunic and brought out a pack of Alas. He offered one to Eliseo and one to Don Concepción. Several of the officials lingered in the doorway of the office, interested, but unable to understand what was going on.

"Yesterday," Don Roberto began after clearing his throat, "an old man named Augustín López Pérez, he was the President once, came to town to tell me his son—a boy named Mario who was the Doctor's assistant—had been shot by some Mexicans while he was trying to find his sheep. Had you heard that, President?"

Oso shook his head and said he had not. Don Concepción's sad old baggy eyes were fixed on Oso's calm face.

"When was this?" Oso asked, as though he were not very interested.

"Three days ago, on Saturday."

"And where did the boy die?"

"On the land behind his house, in the hamlet called Lumtik."

"It isn't possible then, Don Roberto. That land is mine, and there wouldn't be Mexicans on it."

At the other end of the line he could hear Don Roberto let out a sigh. Oso wondered if the whole world was made up of old men without the energy to do the work they had to do. He had never liked Don Roberto, but now he was sorry for him if the lawyer found it so difficult to say whatever it was he had to say next.

"I'm afraid that's not true, Oso. I happened to talk to Don Alonso this morning and he explained that land isn't yours any more, that you sold it to him."

"I *rented* it," Oso said, angry.

"Which you can't do, since the land is part of your ejido."

Oso held the phone closer to his ear and felt the pressure of the cup, hoping the others in the room would no longer be able to hear Don Roberto. Static covered the line for a second.

"But what can I do, Don Roberto?" Oso asked when the connection was clear again. "I don't control what Don Alonso does with his land, or my land. If we knew who the killers were, the Mexicans—but we don't."

"Don Alonso told me it could only be the two men who are working for him there."

"Good. I hope you find them, Don Roberto. Are you going to send police into my territory?" Oso turned with his head toward the wall so the others in the office wouldn't see his smile. "Mexicans who kill Indians—they're for you to find."

"Both of these men were Indians, Oso, revestidos. One of them is your brother Miguel." Don Roberto's voice was strong now, clipped. It had lost its timidity.

"But that's not possible, Don Roberto, my brother is in Flores, he has never worked for Don Alonso."

"Don Alonso says he does."

The others in the room, even Don Concepción, could not help smiling when Oso told the lie about his brother. Oso smiled too, admitting the joke on the lawyer to those present.

"Your brother is there, in your house right now, isn't he, President?"

"No, I haven't seen my brother in a month," Oso said into the receiver. "Who told you that, about my brother?"

"Don Concepción told me right now over the telephone, the Doctor told me when he arrived here at the Institute this morning."

"It was another man, another Mexican who looks like my brother. He was drunk, and I was protecting him." The other men in the room had stopped smiling, and more people had come to the doorway of the office.

Miguel had said once that the thing wrong with the village was its openness, that you couldn't go to San Martín for the day without the village knowing it.

The static was there again, but Don Roberto's voice cracked over it. "If you don't bring your brother to San Martín today, President, when Jacinto's truck comes in, I will take you to Flores to the land commission about selling your ejido."

"Will you take Don Alonso too?"

"Yes."

Oso knew Don Roberto was lying. No one would ever take the richest man in Chiapas, who was also the brother of the Governor, to a land dispute settlement. But Oso believed that Don Roberto would arrest the President of Chomtik.

Though he was angry and already frightened, Oso could think of nothing more to say, and passed the receiver of the telephone back to Don Concepción. He signaled for Eliseo to follow him and they broke through the crowd of old men at the door.

As they were crossing the plaza, moving quickly, Jacinto's truck rounded the curve by the junction with the main road, and began to ease down into the valley. For some reason he did not understand, Oso felt better to see heads pop out of doorways, school children turn to watch the truck come. Some lives here went on with no greater excitement than the arrival of Jacinto in his brilliant red and yellow truck.

22 Don Alonso's Maid

THE NARROW, PAVED STREET before the great house was already dark and quiet though it was not yet quite night, and the clouds over the valley of San Martín, black, showed traces of yellow around the edges, cracking the sky as though lightning had been painted onto the inner dome. The entrance of the great house, though flush to the street, had an awning hanging at a steep angle over it, and was lighted. Through the grill gate was a long pink hallway, bare except for the pots of rubber plants which lined the wall and looked awkwardly tropical. The clouds had closed in during the heat of the day, and only now was there a breeze.

The woman sat waiting on the pavement, moving back against the wall of the house as each person passing looked at her, wondering what an Indian was doing there at this time of the night. The two men stood together on one side of the entrance, away from the light. When the electrical bell tinkling merrily somewhere in the depths of the house failed to bring anyone, the man in the leather jacket and boots rattled the curlicue iron gate. This sound too echoed away and was lost in the absorbing greatness of the house. Oso was mad, and shook again at the bars. Suddenly enough to startle him, a pretty young maid in braids and a pink dress dashed into the hall, laughing, and ran to the entrance.

"To see Don Alonso, Señorita," said Miguel.

"Who is it?" The girl was suspicious.

"The manager of his ranchito in Chomtik."

Without an answer the girl fled down the hall. In a moment the men could hear laughter of Mexicans as doors were opened and closed somewhere. The girl returned, serious, and told them through the bars that Don Alonso had guests for dinner and could not come.

"Tell him it's Miguel, about the sheepstealer."

"And say his brother's here," Juan added.

Peering out, the girl noticed there was an Indian woman with bundles sitting on the sidewalk. "We're not buying anything tonight," the girl said.

"It's not that," Oso explained. "Just tell Don Alonso."

"I can't," the girl whined. "I can't go back and disturb him again."

"Tell him," said Miguel, coughing and looking away, "tell him Miguel and his brother have to have the money to go to Mexico City."

The girl laughed. "And how much would that be?"

"Tell him three hundred pesos."

"Don Alonso doesn't lend money to Indians," the girl said.

"Tell him!" Oso whispered in a low urgent voice. He was caught off balance by this servant calling them Indians.

The girl's smile faded, and she looked half afraid of the harmless strangers on the other side of the bars. After a moment's hesitation, she turned and sauntered away.

The brothers waited, staring down the street, each with his own thoughts. The yellow cracks in the sky had gone, and the dim street lights of San Martín were beginning to glow their ineffective puddles of light in the middle of every block.

Oso's eyes were fixed on the pale-green shiny Mercedes which was parked in front of the house.

When the girl came back, she took two fifty-peso bills from the pocket of her apron and handed them to Miguel. "That's all Don Alonso can give you," she said, not understanding any of the business.

Miguel held the money in the light long enough to let Juan see how much it was, and then tucked it away in his pants.

The girl remained on her side of the grill, waiting to see what else would happen. The two men merely started off down the street and the woman scurried to get up, load on her bundles and follow them. The girl shrugged and bounced off to the kitchen of the great house to finish her supper and gossip with the cook.

23   The Man Salvador

IN THE QUIET OF THE
early evening while the women from his house on the hill
were starting the food, the man Salvador watched his son
coming up toward him through his fields.

The son rested with his father a minute, gratefully ac-
cepting a bowl of corn gruel which his father brought him
from inside.

The boy said he had talked again to the girl he wanted
to ask for in marriage. He knew, he said, that in her heart
the girl wanted to marry, but she still said her father
would beat any boy who came with all his relatives to yell
around the house.

They talked again about going to the Center to get the
President's permission and ask the officials to come along
to the petitioning. They had talked of this before, but Salvador said again that since the President had gone away,
it would be useless to make the trip all the way from Cruztik to the Center. Besides, he had heard that now many
of the officials had gone home. They would have to wait
before beginning any petitions, the father said, appearing
sad.

The boy saw behind his father's face, knew his father
was secretly glad about Juan López Oso's disappearance.
The boy could tell his father was hoping that people in the
Center had forgotten about him and his job as Gobernador.

24   Don Roberto

DON ROBERTO WAS NERVOUS
and shifted uneasily in his chair. He wiped some dust off
his desk with the flat of his big bony hand, then tried to
scan some of the letters which he had left neglected for
over a week. But he couldn't concentrate, and soon returned to watching the sharp thin line of afternoon sun
which cut a diagonal on the wall across from him and was
slowly moving toward Don Roberto's prized old print of
Benito Juárez. The drawing of the great President disturbed Don Roberto when he took the time to look at it
carefully. Juárez seemed caught in a moment of amusement, or possibly of supreme distress. His round cheeks
were drawn up, his eyes hidden. The head was turned
slightly so Juárez never looked at one directly.

Don Roberto could hear trucks going by in the street,
honking, grunting from one low gear to another. The
smooth-running motor of the police van would be recog-
nizable when it drew up before his office, so he needn't be
unprepared.

Don Roberto reached across the desk to his cigarette
box, and opened it. Then he unwrapped the new pack he
had bought for this afternoon and smoked.

He was conscious that though this was a staged affair, a
tiny play, not all of the details could appear contrived to
the man who would be the audience. This man would
have to believe, at least partially, in the reality of it. A new
pack of cigarettes in the box, fresh and unopened, would
be a too-obvious sign.

The lawyer had begun his preparations the preceding Saturday, just ten days after Juan López Oso and his brother ran away. Don Roberto went down to Flores, taking his secretary with him. They went first to the state employment offices, checking through the recent files of work applicants for the names of either of the brothers. By midday they had had no luck. In the afternoon, the lawyer made a tour of the sindicatos, the labor union offices. He was counting on a belief that Oso would not attempt to change his name, and that he had come to Flores, and it was not until after six o'clock that Don Roberto had been proven right. He discovered an applicant named "Juan López" who had, in the previous week, joined Trabajadores Chiapas, and who listed his job as porter at the airport. Don Roberto felt a twinge of excitement when he read the application in Oso's tight, tortured handwriting.

By next morning, Don Roberto had decided on his plan and as part of it he sent his secretary out to the airport. Old Pepe found Oso hauling in the freight luggage from the morning flight from Mexico City and Minatitlán. He caught Oso, and told him that Don Roberto wanted to see him, without mentioning that the lawyer was in Flores. Oso had shrugged off the old man, saying he didn't have the time, and then disappeared in the confusion of the airport.

On Friday a small detachment of state police went to the airport, and Oso was arrested, without any reason being given. He was put in jail overnight, and the Jefe de Policía called Don Roberto on Saturday afternoon right before the blue closed van left Flores.

"He's not a very frightened man," the Jefe de Policía reported to Don Roberto over the phone.

"I know," Don Roberto agreed.

He heard the van pull up outside, and peeked out through the closed window blinds to be sure. Then he went into the adjoining room where his secretary was waiting, impatient.

"They're here. You know what to do?"

"Yes, Don Roberto. I'll meet the police sergeant."

The lawyer went back into his own room, shutting the big double doors behind him. Then he sat down and waited. He could hear the low mumble of voices, then the heavy tramp of feet on the board floors, and a knock at his door.

"What is it, Pepe?" he called.

"The Sergeant of Police from Flores, Don Roberto."

"Come in." Don Roberto sighed as the doors swung open. The sergeant strode into the room, followed by little Pepe. In the doorway there were three policemen with rifles slung over their shoulders, and two of them held ends of the handcuffs which bound Oso at each wrist. The Indian, in Mexican clothes—a white shirt and blue pants —kept his head down.

The Sergeant of Police was a heavy man, and his uniform was tight.

"I have your man, Don Roberto. We found him in Flores."

"What man?" Don Roberto stood up.

"This Juan López you were looking for." The sergeant was ignorant of the lawyer's ruse, since the Jefe in Flores had not trusted his intelligence enough to tell him the story.

"Juan, are you there?" Don Roberto walked around his desk and to the doorway.

Oso looked up. He seemed to have suffered somewhat

from his night in the jail—he was dirty, and his hair was still matted where he had been asleep. But under this, hot country seemed to have done him well. There were slight blotches of red on his cheeks.

"My God, man, what happened? Were you in a fight?"

Oso looked into the Mexican's face, resentful, but would not speak.

Don Roberto turned angrily on the sergeant. "What do you think you're doing?"

"I have an order from you, Don Roberto, to bring an Indian named Juan López to San Martín. I don't know anything more about it." Suddenly the police sergeant lost all of his arrogance, and began to hunt through his inner pockets for the order. He produced it with a flourish, and gave it to the lawyer to read.

Don Roberto took time to read the order, and then turned on his secretary. The secretary could only answer in a confused way that Don Roberto had said he wanted Oso brought to him.

"I said I would like to speak to him if you saw him. Nothing more, you idiot."

Don Roberto was careful to keep the scene in control, for even his secretary, who knew what was going on, was taking his regañada as though it were real.

In the middle of the secretary's long mumbled apology, Don Roberto sharply ordered the police sergeant to take the handcuffs off Oso, and, with his arm around the Indian's shoulder, he brought Oso into the office and put him in the comfortable chair across from his own desk. He opened the cigarette box, and insisted that Oso take one.

"You'll hear about this from the Chief of Police," he promised the befuddled sergeant as he began to push the whole lot of them, including his secretary, out the door.

Once they were gone and the room was quiet again, Don Roberto went to his bookcase and brought out a bottle of rum and a glass he had put there. He poured a drink for Oso, and the other man took it. The lawyer waited until the other man was through drinking. "I'm sorry about this, Juan," he said, sitting down in his own chair.

Oso looked up at him, swallowed the little rum that remained in his mouth, and seemed to be deciding whether or not Don Roberto was really sorry. He didn't say anything.

"How are things going for you?" Don Roberto asked.

There was no answer.

"You're living in Flores then?"

"Yes."

"Do you have work?"

"Yes."

"Where?"

"At the airport, carrying luggage."

"What do you make?"

"Ten pesos a day."

A silence settled over the room as Don Roberto thought how he would say what came next. "You know," he began slowly, "that I am truly sorry about this, and if there's anything I can do for you—"

He was going to say that he would be glad to help Oso in any possible way. But since this unfortunate thing had happened, he was glad they would have a chance to talk. Then he would tell Oso that if the Indian would go back to Chomtik, nothing more would be said about either the ejido or the boy's death. But Don Roberto didn't get his chance.

"Are you sorry?" Oso asked, narrowing his eyes.

"Certainly, I am. You're my friend."

"Then tell them to take me back with them." Oso nodded toward the window. Both men could hear the motor of the police van warming up outside.

"All right," said Don Roberto, with a sigh. "I'll be glad to." He smiled at Oso. Then he got up, and opened the blinds, and told the police sergeant, who was angry himself by now, to take the Indian home to Flores.

Oso put the glass which had held his rum down on the desk, and said, "We'll see you." Then he left the office, and Don Roberto watched him go. The lawyer closed the blinds, so Oso, safe inside the van, wouldn't look back and see his disappointment.

When the sound of the police car was gone, and Don Roberto had dismissed his secretary for the day, he took Oso's glass and had himself a drink of the rum. He was partially satisfied. Oso had gotten away, escaped, before Don Roberto had finished. But at least the moral of the little play should be clear. The Indian knew now where the power was, that the lawyer controlled him. Don Roberto drank his rum calmly.

25 Don Roberto's New Man

BEFORE ANSWERING Don Roberto's question, the Maestro ran his finger across the little mustache he had recently begun to cultivate.

"Well—" he said slowly, looking from Don Roberto to Don Concepción to the schoolboys playing basketball in the plaza, "it's true. In the last two weeks many of the children have stopped coming, but I would not necessarily call that a cause for emergency. In effect—"

Don Roberto cut him off. "How many?"

"Well—there are still some seventy or eighty students, with a regular attendance and—"

"How many missing?" Don Roberto repeatedly jabbed at clots of earth by his foot.

"Thirty or forty," Don Concepción said, since the Maestro seemed hard put to answer.

"Not what we could call an emergency," the Maestro said, leaning back against the fender of the jeep Don Roberto had borrowed from the Institute to drive out to Chomtik.

"How many of the officials are left here in the village?" Don Roberto turned to the Secretary, having to squint into the sun in order to see the old man's face well.

"About half have gone home, I would say."

The Maestro was thinking the others were not treating him right in this important talk. True, he was younger than they were, but he was virtually the Indian Institute's representative in these affairs, and his voice should count. "But, as Don Concepción told you, *he* really runs the business of the village. Just because there is no President at the moment, and the officials have gone home—it doesn't mean anything."

"And there's no court, and no justice either," Don Roberto said, sour, as though the Maestro had interrupted more crucial thoughts.

"After all"—the Maestro appeared knowing—"from time to time all of the officials go home—to bring firewood and corn, et cetera. So basically—"

"What about what people are saying about Carnaval?" Don Roberto asked.

"That's nothing." The Maestro tried to be final about this. He was sorry he had told the story to the lawyer.

Two of his older students told him the day before they had heard from their fathers that the Kanaleros were going to come during the fiesta of Carnaval, to steal the saints. The boys claimed also that the people were afraid, and that many said they would not come themselves to the fiesta. Supposedly the Kanaleros were going to bring their guns, and people would be killed.

The Maestro, though he did not believe the story, of course, had dreamed about it. In the dream the Kanaleros had come, and the Maestro had followed them bravely into the church, to stop them from stealing the saints. But at the moment he was about to become a hero, the people, Chomtikeros, turned on him and began to beat him while the Kanaleros carried off the carved saints.

"It *is* something, if the people believe it," Don Roberto said to the Secretary, almost turning his back on the young schoolteacher. "At least I'll order an extra detachment of police sent out from San Martín at the end of the week, to be on hand for the fiesta."

"Which will frighten the Indians even more," the Maestro broke in.

"What you think, Don Concepción?" the lawyer asked.

"It would certainly be safer with the police."

"And what about the Presidency? Will the Indians pick someone else, or can you do it?"

Don Roberto was looking for answers, and for a moment Don Concepción weighed both of these possibilities with great seriousness. "No," he said finally, "I just don't have that power. No, the Indians will get themselves a new President if Oso doesn't come back—but you can't expect them to move quickly. No." It took the Secretary a long time to hunt for and find the right words when he was being so serious and judicious.

"I see." Don Roberto began again to pace up and down in front of the green jeep, while the other two Mexicans watched him. "Well," he said at last, stopping in his stride, "maybe we'll talk about this some more. Now I'm going to drink a beer." There was nothing frivolous about Don Roberto, and neither of the other men even ventured a smile.

The Maestro excused himself to supervise the game of basketball his older boys were playing, and Don Concepción went back inside the Cabildo.

Don Roberto paced and thought of the alternatives open to him. As usual he laid them out like empty boxes in his mind, and tried filling each with the ingredients of his problem. But this time none of the boxes seemed big enough to contain the whole matter. So, thinking of all the possibilities about as seriously as he was thinking what the good effects of a beer would be, he crossed the plaza to Jacinto's store, casting a long, grotesque shadow before him in the dust as he went.

The old President's son Eliseo was sitting on the stoop of the store gently stroking slightly incorrect chords from his Mexican guitar. Sitting this way he reminded Don Roberto to a painful extent of his own eldest son, who was a failure at the University in Mexico City, but a good guitar player. Eliseo was a handsome boy for an Indian, Don Roberto thought, and then he wondered if his feeling was based on his knowledge that the boy was brighter than most. Looking again, Don Roberto decided the boy was not so much handsome as intelligent.

"Ho, Eliseo."

"Ho!" The boy seemed surprised to see the tall lawyer, though he must have noticed the jeep arrive in the village an hour earlier. Eliseo came to the man and shook his

hand. Like a Mexican, not an Indian. He must have
learned the other way, the heartiness, from his father,
Don Roberto decided. Also the forthrightness, the lack
of servility.

"Is there any beer, Eliseo?"

Eliseo leaned his guitar against one of the supports of
the porch. "Right now I'll bring it, Patrón." He smiled.

Patrón, the old word the Indians used with Mexicans.
Don Roberto was surprised to hear it, and Eliseo laughed.
"Bring one for yourself too, boy," the lawyer said.

The beer was warm, but Don Roberto enjoyed it, since
the day had been hot and discouraging and the road to
Chomtik a cloud of dust. He sat down where Eliseo had
been.

"You didn't want to work for me, then," the Mexican
said.

"What work is that?" asked Eliseo.

"I told your father once I would train you as my secretary in town, if you wanted."

"I don't write well—I can't use a typewriter."

The Indian's customary self-effacement, thought Don
Roberto. It was especially unconvincing coming from this
boy.

"But you speak good Spanish, and you speak Tzotzil,
and that's all my secretary really has to do. My old man
wants to quit. But if you didn't want to, I knew you must
have had your reasons."

"My father never told me."

"Well," Don Roberto said, remembering the old President's puzzled face, "then your father must have had his
reasons, huh?"

"Yes," Eliseo replied hesitantly.

Don Roberto had been having his peculiar brand of fun,

playing with other people to see how they would react. He had not cared especially about Eliseo and the job of secretary—there were plenty of bright young Indians at the schools in town, more knowledgeable than this boy. Yet Don Roberto wondered why the old President who died had not wanted his own son to have this work. Unless there had not been time to tell the boy.

"How long ago did your father die, Eliseo?" Don Roberto remained casual.

"Thirty days ago."

"And the day before he died, what did he do?"

"He came to San Martín to see you, about the boy who killed his father."

"But he was sick when he returned from town that day?"

"Yes, he was already sick."

Don Roberto thought another moment, then smiled at the boy. "It must have been that day I asked him to talk to you about working for me. Would you want that, Eliseo?"

Eliseo grinned and shrugged his shoulders.

The other candidates Don Roberto had thought of for the job would have admitted readily they wanted the work. "Your father seemed to want it, Eliseo."

"Well, then, we'll see, Señor."

It was noncommittal, but from the speed of the reply Don Roberto knew the boy had agreed, so he stood up and shook hands.

"Will you start for me tomorrow?" he asked suddenly.

"I would have to tell Jacinto to find someone else to watch his store."

Don Roberto squinted, so his gaunt face was almost angry-looking. "But can you start for me tomorrow? I have a trip that must be made."

"Where are you going, Señor?"

"Not me—I want you to go alone, to Flores, to talk to Juan López Oso. Will you do that?" The Mexican handed his empty beer bottle back to the boy.

"But Señor, there is the problem that no one knows where Oso is."

Don Roberto put on a look of surprise. "You don't know?"

"No."

"He's working at the airport there. Do you know Flores? Where the airport is?"

"I've been there to see it."

"All right. Tomorrow go there and tell Oso that the matter of the boy and Don Alonso's land is forgotten—and then ask him to come back." Don Roberto hid his excitement with discovering a new box which would, at least temporarily, contain the whole tangled problem.

"Do you understand, Eliseo?"

"Yes, Señor."

"All right, here's money then." Don Roberto fished into his pocket and pulled out fifty pesos in bills; then he gave the boy change for the beer. "And come to see me after you get back—stay overnight in Flores if you want to—but come to see me whenever you arrive in San Martín, even if it's at night, come to my house."

Eliseo nodded, and then they shook hands again.

A trip to Flores for whatever reason was excitement enough for him, so he began to think about that. The possibility of work in San Martín—he believed Don Roberto's offer, but it was still too remote to think about.

26   Eliseo

JACINTO LEFT EARLY
the next morning, seven o'clock, on the first trip into San
Martín. His only passenger was Eliseo, who also rode in
the cab, and who kept an even stare on the road, trying to
avoid having to talk.

"What's wrong?" Jacinto asked, as they cleared the top
of the valley above the village. "Didn't you sleep?"

In fact, Eliseo had not slept, much at any rate, because
Jacinto had been screwing his wife the night before, and
Eliseo could hear them in the dark. In the beginning,
always, Jacinto would go slow, but as it went on Jacinto
must have lost patience with his attempt to make no
noise, and the creakings of the plank bed and finally the
snorts of the two people were too much for Eliseo.

"What's Don Roberto want you to go to Flores for?"
Jacinto said when he got no answer for his first question.

"I don't know."

"What's he paying you?"

"I don't know."

A grin spread on Jacinto's almost perfectly round fat
face, but Eliseo did not even respond to that. Let Jacinto
think he was being cheated.

It was eight-fifteen by Eliseo's watch when they got to
San Martín and the street was lined with trucks—some
like Jacinto's from the Indian towns, others unloading
goods from hot country. On the block-long raft of steps
where anyone could sell, women were laying out their
goods on shawls. It was not really time yet, but the streets

were crowded and the market record player was already booming music and bargains.

"Where do I get the bus for Flores? Here?" Eliseo asked when Jacinto had parked the truck.

"You're really going then?"

"Yes."

"Huh." Jacinto had not believed before that it was true. "There on the street out of town beyond the parque."

Without any more words Eliseo climbed down from the cab of the truck, crossed the street, and began threading his way between people toward the parque. Indians from Kanal, Kishin, his own Chomtikeros—a man trying to sell the pine coffin strapped on his back—Ladinos talking, selling bottles or chunks of candied fruit. Eliseo hurried.

It was clear now and beginning to turn warm. In the open parque where the old bandstand was, Eliseo bought a plastic tube of sherbet, ripped off the end with his teeth, and sucked as he went on toward the bus station on a side street. There in the confusion of snorting buses, luggage, baskets, boxes being loaded, he bought a second-class ticket to Flores for six pesos.

There was a bus at nine and another at ten, so Eliseo lined up for the first one. He was near the end of the line, and passed the time until the bus began to load talking to an old man from Santa María who was going to Flores, to have an operation at the clinic. The old man made Eliseo feel better, since he was so openly afraid about his journey.

Eliseo took off his hat as he handed his ticket to the bus driver, a burly man with thick hands and a cigarette in his mouth.

"No, this is the ten o'clock bus," the man said without looking up.

Eliseo glanced at the ticket, which had "Salida a las 9" written on it. He showed this to the driver, with his finger by the 9.

The man said, "Not enough room, your ticket doesn't have a seat number."

Below "Salida a las 9" the ticket read "Número 36." Eliseo held it up again.

"At ten, I said!" the driver grumbled out loud. People already on the bus turned from stowing their packages in the racks, poked their heads out the open windows to see what had happened.

Eliseo stepped aside, and the driver tore off half the old man's ticket and helped him up the steps. "Fucking Indians."

The old man heard it too, and from inside looked out at Eliseo. He didn't say anything.

When the bus pulled out Eliseo watched and thought himself lucky—it was over-crowded, people had to stand.

They gave him space on the bus an hour later. In that time he had gone to a dry goods store and bought a pair of dark blue cotton pants. From the fat lady with the steely eye who ran the store he begged permission to change his pants in the back. She was used to this performance and tolerated it with a thin smile.

As he walked back to the bus station, Eliseo continually looked down to see his pants. They tickled his legs and made him feel cold as though a breeze were touching him. In a store next to the station he bought an emptied sugar bag, folded his white tunic and put it inside. This would be better anyway, Eliseo thought, since it would be uncomfortably hot for the wool tunic once he got to Flores.

The ten o'clock bus was not so full, and Eliseo settled back to take the ride with calm pleasure.

When they got to Flores, the road widened, and great street lights on long slender poles bent toward the bus. Past the army base and the government corn sheds, stacked high with bags at this time of year. Then greenery. The palm-shaded yards of rich Flores businessmen, their American cars tucked in by their pastel modern houses.

Eliseo stared out at the office buildings and yellow stone squares with fountains, the open-front restaurants from which poured the smell of freshly roasted coffee. Politicians and lawyers sat in the cafes.

Eliseo had been here before, with his father. On the street outside the bus station dust caught in his throat, and he walked along holding his kerchief over his mouth. An old lady pointed out the road to the airport, and showed him where to wait for the bus that went there, but after a few minutes' impatience, Eliseo started out along the highway on foot. It was already afternoon and here in hot country stores had begun to close up for the midday rest.

When he was in the outskirts of the other side of town, in a poor section where the houses were adobe, Eliseo realized how hungry he was, and bought six fat bananas for a peso. He ate as he walked, and wondered what could have drawn Oso to this hot place.

The airport was apart from the city, off the highway and beyond a workers' section where the women, in long shiny skirts, came out of their one-room houses and stared after Eliseo. A cab passed by, going to the airport, and then another. Finally Eliseo came in sight of the building, a long low yellow one in the middle of a field, with a tower beside it. There seemed no way to get inside except through the glass front doors. Inside it was cooler and there was music. Eliseo waited, wondering where Oso

would be, then thinking he was not here and Don Roberto
had been wrong.

There was a burly man in a rumpled khaki uniform
standing against the wall. Eliseo could tell the man was
watching him, and he began to expect they would throw
him out.

"What is it?"

"I'm looking for a man named Juan López Oso."

"Does he owe you money?"

"No."

"Juan Lopez, huh? Go through that door and look
around the corner."

"Good. Thank you."

"His name is Juan López, isn't it? The man you're looking for?"

"Yes."

"All right, over there then."

Eliseo went out through the other glass doors, the ones
leading to the runway and the planes, onto a grassed
patio; there was no one in sight. He went to one corner
of the building and peered around it. Leaning against the
yellow wall was a wooden shed, crammed with boxes and
packages. Two men sat inside eating tortillas, and one of
them was Oso.

"Ho," he called. He got up with his food still in his hand
and came out to meet Eliseo. Oso was wearing clothes
almost like Eliseo's—baggy blue worker's pants and a
white shirt. But instead of huaraches he was wearing the
shiny black boots he had shown Eliseo when he came back
to Chomtik after the first trip to Flores.

Oso seemed thinner, darker, perhaps he had been sick.
He brought Eliseo into the shed, sat him down on a

luggage cart, and shared his meal with the boy—tortillas, cold beans and a bottle of water. The other man was a Mexican, who smelled heavily of sweat and didn't speak. When he finished his lunch he got up and left. It was only then that Oso spoke in Tzotzil.

"Well," he said, leaning back and taking out a pack of cigarettes, "you're here."

"Yes."

"Are you going to stay?"

"No, I came to look around."

"Good." Oso put a cigarette in his own mouth and offered one to Eliseo.

"How is it here? Are you feeling good?" Eliseo asked.

"Yes. It is good. I'm making money."

"The work hard?"

"Yes."

They heard footsteps and a Mexican with a round head and tiny mustache came around the corner. His thin white shirt was mapped with dark splotches of sweat and he carried a clipboard.

"Ho, Juan!" he called. "Let's get ready to load."

Oso laughed. "You see? Hard." He sprang to his feet and started out of the shed. "Come watch."

Eliseo followed out into the bright light. The airport had filled with happy laughing people—men going to Mexico City on business trailed by their obese, giggling wives and many tiny children. Eliseo stood out of the way and watched Oso as he put tags on the luggage, put it on his cart, and took it out to the spot on the runway where the plane would pull up.

Eliseo watched Oso carefully. The man worked like an Indian, not like a Ladino. Again and again he threw himself at it, lifting, hauling. Between strokes, when he breathed, he smiled. Not like a Mexican, the Mexican never used all his energy at once.

Yet Oso didn't work quite like an Indian. Every few minutes an Indian would rest. And Oso did not until the plane came in.

Oso and the other porter were the first to race toward it, pushing their carts before them. Another man followed with stairs.

Eliseo lost sight of his friend for a while as Mexicans got off the plane and others left their families to board it. But when the plane was shut up again and the stairs came away, Oso appeared at Eliseo's side, hot and smiling.

"Watch now," he whispered in Spanish.

As if following Oso's voice the plane began to turn slowly and moved back toward the runway. The motors grew loud and troubled again, and Eliseo remembered the times he had been the best schoolboy runner and had gone to San Martin to race against the Ladinos. He remembered the moment before the race began when he drew everything up into himself.

Without a signal the plane started running, and dipped out of sight, as though hiding its secret; when it appeared again it was already small and flashed against the mountains.

Later, after the sun was gone and the day already cooler, they were walking to Oso's house when the older man said, "Inside, it smells like gasoline and oil for lamps, all mixed."

Eliseo had been thinking of other things—how Oso could want to live here in Flores with all the heat and the flies.

"What?"

"The plane, it smells of fine gasoline and oil."

"And where the people ride?"

"Like a bus, but finer."

"Do you know how to drive it yet?"

"Not yet." Oso laughed and Eliseo laughed with him, since the older man was bragging.

The place Oso had found to live was a small room behind a poor Mexican's house, not far from the airport. Oso's woman was there, tending a small fire in the middle of the room. Eliseo expected to see Juan's brother, Miguel, but he did not appear.

They sat by the doorway and drank water the woman brought them and watched the Mexican's children playing with a scrawny chicken. Oso's woman looked cleaner, she wore her hair braided in two strands which were tied together with a ribbon.

"You come to stay, then?" asked Oso.

"No. I'll go back tomorrow."

"Came to look around."

"Yes, and I brought a message from the lawyer."

"Which lawyer?"

"Don Roberto."

Oso snorted. "Oh—his secretary came to see me."

"He did?" Eliseo was surprised. He wondered then what reason Don Roberto had for him to make another trip. Oso must know already that the lawyer wanted to forgive the thing about Mario's death. But Eliseo recited the message anyway.

"What does that mean?" Oso asked.

"I don't know," said Eliseo.

"Here, will you drink something?" Oso got up and started into the house.

"What for?" called Eliseo.

"To warm our hearts. Because you've come." Oso returned with a half-empty bottle of yellow Comiteco and a glass. He put the bottle at Eliseo's feet.

Eliseo gazed at the strong stuff. "Do you need to warm your heart in hot country?" he asked.

Oso smiled and accepted the full glass Eliseo poured for him. "Your heart can be tired anywhere," he said, and drained the glass.

When Eliseo had drunk and the woman had been handed her copita, Eliseo risked his question. "Isn't Miguel here?"

"No," said Oso, "he went to Mexico City." Oso seemed happy about this.

"Didn't you want to go too?"

"Yes. But there was only enough money for one."

"Couldn't you go now though?"

Oso shrugged, he had no answer. They drank again and then went inside to eat. Then Oso laid down a straw mat between the doorway and the remains of the fire—near the door for the breeze, and near the smoke to keep away the mosquitoes, he said, and Eliseo got ready to sleep there. Oso blew out the lamp.

"What's going on in the village?" he asked in the dark.

"Nothing. Nothing's going on."

"Who's the new President?"

"There isn't one."

"Didn't the officials choose one?"

"No, most of them have gone home."

"Huh. Then the Institute should get someone—or Don Roberto. Or maybe Don Roberto would like in his heart to do it himself. They say his mother was an Indian."

In the dark Eliseo laughed with Oso.

"And what's your friend Jacinto doing?" Oso asked a few minutes later.

"He's screwing his wife, since you left."

Oso laughed again. "And you, have you found your woman?"

"No, I don't have any money to pay for a wife."

"I'll give you one of mine."

Eliseo could hear the woman in the plank bed with Oso was saying something, but he could not tell what.

They were up early in the morning since Oso had to get to his work and Eliseo wanted to buy things in the market before taking the bus back up the mountains to San Martín.

27   Second Alcalde

FROM THE MARKET STEPS, cool in the shade of trees, he looked down on the street and the line of stores facing it. Black dressed old Mexican women moved along slowly, one old lady paused briefly beside two dusty Kishineros who were selling peanuts from the burlap bags spread before them.

Jauntily, the Second Alcalde went down the steps and faced the pink façade of the Church of the Merced. Passing, he took off his hat. Behind the church was the low arch, the blue entrance to the prison of Santo Domingo. Mexican soldiers guarded it, one with a rifle, the other resting, digesting his lunch. The Second Alcalde carried a sack and a net bag over one shoulder. He put down the sack while he was thinking of what to say to the soldiers.

"There's a boy inside. I came to talk to him."

The bigger soldier put down his gun. "No, too late. Come in the morning."

"But I came from a long way, Patrón."

"Is he your son?"

The Second Alcalde's little mustache bristled when he smiled. "Yes, sir, it's my son," he lied.

The soldiers exchanged glances and shrugged. "In there. If he's not out in the courtyard, you'll have to come back another time."

"Thank you, Patrón." The Second Alcalde bowed and briefly took off his hat to the soldiers. He picked up his sack and hurried through the archway into the familiar cement courtyard. More soldiers here, lounging on benches, talking so their voices echoed off the high walls. A small group of black-haired prisoners in denim shirts took turns playing with a top. Others sat in lines, their backs against the wall, weaving bright colored thread into pieces of embroidery. The Second Alcalde recognized a man he had known when he was serving his own term. The man was being taught how to write by the boy sitting beside him. They were Chomtikeros, but like all the other prisoners they wore the nondescript cotton clothing the Mexicans gave them. The Second Alcalde greeted the man learning to write. He had been put in jail for killing a witch in his hamlet.

When the little official moved down the line of men looking for his friend, some of the prisoners looked up at him and mutely offered whatever they were making, in case he wanted to buy.

The boy was sitting apart, in a place where a shaft of the afternoon sun still heated the wall. He was intent on rolling fiber into cord, rolling with the flat of his hand against a piece of leather strapped to his thigh.

The Second Alcalde set down his sack.

"Nothing," the boy said without looking up. "I don't have the money today."

The Alcalde laughed and the boy glanced up. "I'm sorry," the boy said, getting to his feet. "I thought you were selling." Quickly he bowed and the Alcalde released him with his right hand. Together they squatted against the wall. The boy went back to rolling his string.

"How is it?"

"Good enough. I sold the first bag, to the wife of a man from San Pedro."

"How much did she give you?"

"Four pesos. It wasn't a very good bag."

The Second Alcalde considered and watched the boy, pleased with his skill. The boy selected several new fibers from a pile beside him and began to roll them into the string, up and down the length of his thigh.

"I bought food with the money."

"Good." The official took his own net bag from his shoulder and began to rummage inside it. At last he took out black, sticky little overripe bananas. He held them together in his hand, there were five in all, and he picked pieces of lint from them. "Will you take these?" he asked, handing them to the boy.

"Thank you, Alcalde." The boy bowed his head and the older man touched him.

"I didn't have money for more—I spent what I had at the fiesta."

"How was it?"

The Alcalde sighed and looked around him. He longed to have something to do with his hands.

"Not good at first. Nobody was there on Friday or Saturday. The people were afraid because there was no President and they didn't come. The officials weren't there, they were afraid too." He watched the boy's work for a moment. "Roll the cord tighter," he said.

"Yes, Alcalde. Where was the President, the new one?"

"Who knows? He had been gone a long time, no one knows where. The Mexican soldiers came from San Martín and watched the market, so no one was selling liquor. Some people said the soldiers were going to steal the saints and the bell from the church and burn the church again. They burned it once when I was a little boy." He found a chip of gravel and began to rub it against the cement.

"I was home in my hamlet and on Sunday I said to my wife, 'Let's go to the fiesta,' and she said no, she was afraid, so I told her to come along but to leave the children to guard our house. So we went, because it was the fiesta of Carnaval."

"Were the *pasiones* there and the *mash*?"

"Yes, they ran in the plaza with their flags but there was almost no one to watch them, the people were afraid and stayed in the hills away from the Center. Then on Monday I said to my wife, 'Let's go home, this is not a real fiesta. No one to drink with.' We were on the road when Jacinto's truck came and in the front part I saw Juan López Oso, sitting with the Mexican who takes us to court. The tall one."

"Don Roberto."

"Yes, him. They came to the plaza and the new President went to his store and got his hat with the ribbons and his black tunic and his cane with the silver tip. Then he came out and went to the church to pray to San Juan. I ran to my house in the village and got my black clothes and went to the church too. All the people had heard the President was back and they came down from the hills to see and weren't afraid any more."

The boy's hands were still as he listened.

"I got into the church but my wife didn't, there were so many people. Well then, the President came outside and in front of the church he stopped and read the speech. The one they say at Carnaval."

"And the people stopped being afraid."

"Yes. Then after that the *mash* put down the grass in the plaza as they always do on the Monday of Carnaval and lit it and then the *pasiones* and the *mash* ran on the fire. And Juan López Oso ran too and some of the officials ran too because they were drunk.

"Then the President said to Don Roberto, 'Look,' he said, 'I'm the President here, the people aren't afraid, take your soldiers away.' And Don Roberto said, 'All right, if the people aren't afraid,' and he went away with his soldiers in Jacinto's truck."

The boy nodded.

"Then everybody got drunk, all the *mash* and the people, even the women. Everybody was shouting and fighting and the *pasiones* ran some more in the plaza and exploded their fireworks."

The little official felt cold. The warm swatch of sun was gone from the wall of the prison.

"Will you take a little drink?" he asked the boy. "For the cold?"

The Second Alcalde got up and squatted again before his sack with his back to the courtyard. In the sack were piles of sugar-covered rolls which made the boy hungry. The Alcalde at last found his bottle. "Here," he said, handing it to the boy. "Go on and drink. There's no glass."

The boy leaned forward after unstopping the bottle and the official touched his head.

"Go on and drink, Alcalde." The boy passed him the bottle.

"I'll take it," the Alcalde said, looking around to be sure the soldiers were not watching.

He handed the bottle to the boy, who sipped from it. "Go on, take more."

"Thank you, Alcalde."

The liquor was strong and the boy's eyes were wet when at last he handed the bottle back.

"I have to go, it's going to be dark," the Alcalde said as he stowed the bottle in his sack.

"Are you taking Jacinto's truck?"

"No, walking. I don't have the peso for the truck."

Halfway across the courtyard he turned and looked at the boy, who had returned to rolling his fiber. The Second Alcalde beamed at the guards as he came out of the archway, took off his hat to them, adjusted his net bag and threw the sack over his other shoulder. The street leading out of San Martín was empty.

GLOSSARY

GLOSSARY

The terms in *italics* are Tzotzil, rendered in Spanish orthography. Spanish terms used in the book often have unusual and specific use in Chamula ("Chomtik").

Alcalde: an appointed lesser official of the town government

barrio: usually, a neighborhood, a district, or a geographical division; Chamula is composed of three large barrios

Cabaña: here, the regional station and center for the Indian Institute

Cabildo: town hall

cabrón: a male goat; an epithet equivalent in force to "son of a bitch" in English

Carnaval: a major religious festival which precedes Lent

Center: the village proper within the township; location of church, market, stores, government buildings

chanul: animal spirit of a human being; a person's *chanul* is said to live in the world as long as he or she does

comal: a flat round griddle of metal or clay used mainly to cook tortillas

Comiteco: a brand of yellowish liquor manufactured in Chiapas

cruda: hangover

curer: a nonmedical practitioner or healer who knows how to divine which parts of a person's soul are lost and how to intercede with spirits and deities for their recovery

ejido: common land; since the Mexican Revolution, land ceded by the government to towns and distributed to individuals; generally, ejido land is inherited by eldest sons and may not be sold or rented

finca: plantation; in Chiapas, large estates in hot country, many given over to raising coffee and using migrant labor

Gobernador: an appointed official of the town government

hamlet: a country living area; in Spanish, paraje; the homes and fields of a group of families, often defined by a valley or other geographical divider

hkashlan: a Tzotzil loan word from the Spanish "castellano"; a non-Indian, a foreigner

ik'al (pl. *ik'aletik*): winged and evil night creatures, capable of stealing women and sheep

Institute, Indian Institute: the Instituto Nacional Indigenista (INI); a service organization devoted to education, health care improvement, land reclamation and agricultural advance in the principal Indian areas of Mexico

Ladino: a nonIndian, a mestizo, a person who wears western clothes and speaks Spanish

lastimó: a pity, a shame; a Tzotzil loan word from Spanish

mano and metate: a stone grinding pin and a sloping stone trough, used for grinding corn

masa: corn dough

mash: men dressed in soldier costume, including peaked fur hats, at fiestas, especially Carnaval; *mash* may play instruments, or menace the crowd with whips; some have official duties; thought of as dangerous, licentious, or merely funny; the word also means "monkey"

Mayor: the lowest of the appointed civil officials; Mayores serve as policemen, guards, and messengers

Paludismo: malaria

pasión: an important religious official, responsible for rituals in major fiestas, especially Carnaval

patrón: master, lord, boss

posh: colorless, usually strong liquor, distilled from cake brown sugar

regañada: a scolding, a reprimand

revestido: literally, "redressed"; a person of changed clothing and habit; an Indian who has become a Ladino

San Juan: Saint John, the patron of Chamula

San Jermino: (dim. of Jerónimo), Saint Jerome; in Chamula, the patron saint of the sick, and of lost souls

San Sebastián: Saint Sebastian; in Chamula a shepherd, and the watcher of sheep; second only to San Juan in importance

Scribe: Spanish, escribano; a regular town official; usually a young man who knows how to write; Scribes assist the President, especially in elections and census-taking

Síndico: a minor official in the town government

sitio: the yard surrounding a house, usually fenced, or the earth terrace before a house

Torino: a brand of sweet red vermouth

tumpline: a rope, sometimes padded or fitted with a flat leather section, worn across the forehead and attached to heavy loads carried on the back

trago: a drink; also liquor